C

The Conway's have more than 1.2 million books in print in 14 different languages.

- **Men In Midlife Crisis**
- **Your Husband's Midlife Crisis**
- **Women In Midlife Crisis**
- **Maximize Your Midlife**
- **Friendship – Making Real Friends In A Phony World**
- **Your Marriage Can Survive Midlife Crisis**
- **What God Gives When Life Takes/Trusting God In A Family Crisis**
- **Menopause – Help and hope for this passage**
- **Adult Children Of Legal Or Emotional Divorce**
- **Traits Of A Lasting Marriage**
- **When A Mate Wants Out**
- **Sexual Harassment No More**
- **Pure Pleasure**
- **Moving On After He Moves Out**

The Conways are also contributors to:

- **How To Get Your Teenager To Talk To You**
- **How To Raise Christian Kids In A Non-Christian World**
- **The Making Of A Marriage**
- **Men's Devotional Bible:** *Daily Devotions From Godly Men, The New International Version*
- **The Resource Guide For Christian Counselors**
- **Friendship Is A Special Gift**
- **Couples' Devotional Bible, New International Version,**

Zondervan
- **The Family Life Bible, The New Living Bible, Tyndale**
- **The Marriage You've Always Wanted**

The Conway's website www.midlife.com, gives information about each book, and how you may purchase a copy.

SALLY CONWAY, MS
JIM CONWAY, PHD

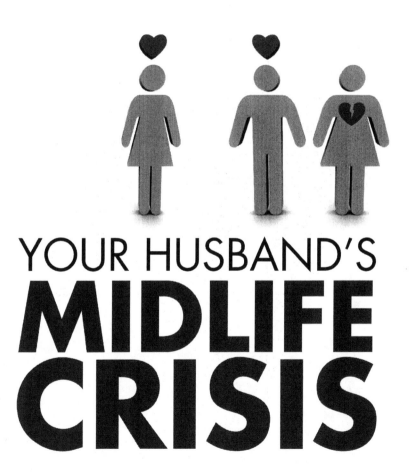

YOUR HUSBAND'S
MIDLIFE
CRISIS

Your Husband's Midlife Crisis

Published by:
Intermedia Publishing Group, Inc.
P.O. Box 2825
Peoria, Arizona 85380
www.intermedia pub.com

ISBN 978-1-935529-82-8

Copyright © 2010 by Jim Conway
Printed in the United States of America

No part of this publication may be reproduced, stored in a retrieval system, or transmitted in any form by any means – electronic, mechanical, digital photocopy, recording, or any other without the prior permission of the author.

All rights reserved solely by the author. The author guarantees all contents are original and do not infringe upon the legal rights of any other person or work. No part of this book may be reproduced in any form without the permission of the author.

Copyright © 1980, Sally Conway (formerly, *You and Your Husband's Midlife Crisis),* Copyright © 1987 (With a Bible Study), Published by David C. Cook Publishing Co. Printed in the United States of America

Unless otherwise indicated, all Scripture quotations are taken from the Holy Bible, New Living Translation, copyright © 1996. Used by permission of Tyndale House Publisher's, Inc., Wheaton, IL 60189. All rights reserved.

Library of Congress Cataloging in Publication Data
Conway, Jim; Conway, Sally
Your Husband's Midlife Crisis

Includes bibliographical references.
1. Midlife crisis, 1. Climacteric, Male. 2. Menopause. I. Title

RC884.c66 612'.665 80-23863

LIFE WITH A MIDLIFE MAN

Your husband's midlife crisis may cause you some of the greatest stress you have ever experienced.

- You will be shocked to see him question values and choices you thought had been settled long ago.

- You will have trouble understanding why he is so preoccupied with his aging.

- When he accuses you of being the cause of his problems or gives you the cold, silent treatment, you will feel rejected and misunderstood.

These days will likely be anxious and confusing for both of you. But if your husband successfully integrates the conflicts raging within him, a better life lies ahead for both of you – and your marriage.

As the wife of a midlife husband you need to know the basic facts, the resources available to you, and what you can do to help your husband through this most difficult of times.

Jim and Sally have spoken on five continents, and frequently appeared on radio and television – including the Conways' daily radio program on 200 stations. They have both taught at several Universities or Colleges. They are parents of 3 daughters, and grandparents of 12 grandchildren.

Sally Conway, M.S., was vice president of **Christian Living Resources, Inc./Midlife Dimensions**. She authored or co-authored 12 books such as *When a Mate Wants Out*, *Moving on After He Moves Out*, and *Traits of a Lasting Marriage*. Sally died in 1997, after a 7 year battle with breast cancer.

Jim Conway, Ph.D., holds two masters degrees and two doctorates. He is the president of **Christian Living Resources, Inc./Midlife Dimensions**, an international counseling and conference ministry. In addition to revising the current edition of this book, Jim has authored 15 other books, including his best seller, "*Men in Midlife Crisis*".

Continued public demand for this book, "*Your Husband's Midlife Crisis*", has encouraged Jim to make a full revision.

In 2006, Jim married Jan Kinne, a missionary with YWAM – after her husband died of cancer in 2000. Jan is the author of, "The Finisher, A New Path for Your Second Half". Jim and Jan continue to teach, led conferences, counsel, write, and speak on radio and TV.

To Jim,

*whose entire life as my husband
has been a living example
of the sacrificial love and
servanthood of Christ,* **and**
*whose midlife storm taught us both
more about vulnerable living and loving.*

(Sally's original dedication)

CONTENTS

Foreword   I

PART ONE
YOUR HUSBAND'S MIDLIFE CRISIS
1. Coming Unglued   3
2. They Never Warned Me!   9
3. Why So Much at One Time?   17
4. But Who Cares about Me?   27

PART TWO
YOUR DILEMMA
5. Life of a Midlife Wife   35
6. Life with a Midlife Man   43
7. Life in a Triangle   53
8. Life without Him   71
9. Life with the Children   93

PART THREE
HELP FOR YOU
10. Peace That Empowers   107
11. Strength, Stability, Sanity   121
12. Dependence, Independence, or Interdependence?   135
13. The Friendship Connection   151
14. Older, But Better!   165

PART FOUR
HELPING YOUR HUSBAND
15. Winning Attitudes   187
16. Understanding His Needs   205
17. Helping Him Win   215

| 18 | Aiding His Reentry | 233 |
| 19 | You Can Do This! | 243 |

PART FIVE
Chapter Notes   251

FOREWORD

Always Midlife Crisis

For the past thirty years, an endless stream of telephone calls, email, and letters have come to us from women all across the country, as well as Canada, and other countries. They usually begin by saying, "Your book, **Men in Midlife Crisis**, exactly describes my husband. I was ready to give up on our marriage, but after reading the book I now understand what is happening to my husband is something temporary."

The next comments usually describe their situation. Even though the names and places are different, again and again we have heard the same story of a husband struggling desperately with the meaning of life, perhaps an affair – and the marriage falling apart.

In great pain women ask, "How can I survive this horrible experience?" "I understand I need to meet my husband's needs, *but who meets my needs?*"

Other questions also pour out such as – "What do I tell the children?" "Should I force him to choose between me and the other woman?" "How can I save our marriage?" "Should I move out of the house?" "Should I kick him out of the house?" "What should I tell our parents?" "How much should I change to please him?"

Sally and I have spent hundreds of hours leading conferences, on radio and TV programs, plus counseling through email, letters, and long-distance telephone calls around the world. Many times we answer the same questions answered in previous letters or calls. Even though the questions are the same – the intense pain is each woman's personal "Hell."

This book is written to answer the questions of women whose husbands are going through Midlife Crisis – plus give hope in the midst of a desert of hopelessness.

As we began to see a growing need for this book, Sally and I collected data through a nationwide survey which would help us to more fully understand the problems women were experiencing and to learn their sources of strength. The information from this national survey, and from personal correspondence and counseling, has been integrated into this book as real, live situations, but with the names changed.

About the Authors

SALLY CONWAY, M.S.

Sally was a woman who always was involved in leadership, from her high school days as class president and valedictorian, to community organizations, as a pastor's wife, and as a public school reading specialist. Later, she took on new careers of editing and writing books, and became a conference speaker on topics such as child development, marriage and family, Christian womanhood, and "Midlife Crisis."

Women frequently sought her about how she was able to be such an effective mother to our three daughters, wife to me, a pastor's wife in churches, a professor at Biola University, write books, do radio and TV, co-found Midlife Dimensions – plus be a terrific grandmother.

Sally managed changes and responsibilities because she had a deep, personal relationship with Christ enabling her to rise above the stress of life. One of our family memories is Sally sitting by the living room window each morning reading her Bible. Her connection with God gave her the edge – and the power.

JIM CONWAY, D.Min., PH.D.

President, Christian Living Resources Inc., Midlife Dimensions

Author, conference speaker, graduate professor, and counselor:

Jim Conway served as a pastor for over 25 years and then for 5 years was The Director of the Doctor of Ministry program and Associated Professor at Talbot School of Theology, Biola University, California. He holds 5 earned degrees in theology and psychology is listed in "Who's Who," and "Men of Achievement." Jim has written 15 books, such as *Men In Midlife Crisis*, *Women In Midlife Crisis*, and *Traits Of A Lasting Marriage*, plus hundreds of magazine articles.

It is Jim's hope that women will not only receive credible information, but also be pointed to the strength available through a vital relationship with God. The goal of this book is that women's lives will be healed, marriages restored, churches strengthened, and, society made more whole.

Part One
Your Husband's Midlife Crisis

SALLY CONWAY, M.S. • JIM CONWAY, D.Min., PH.D.

1

COMING UNGLUED

My husband angrily grabbed his coat and slammed out the door. My heart was smashed on the floor, where it had been so often lately. But I thought we recently had been doing better. Yes, he still seemed depressed and confused much of the time, but generally he didn't blame me as much anymore.

As I watched Jim walk away down the snowy drive, I realized I had been off guard this evening. I had nagged a little bit and questioned an insignificant decision he'd made. Until a few months ago he would have let these small remarks go unchallenged. He was the one with the wide shoulders and the uncritical spirit. But now he had become hypersensitive, and I had to measure my words and reactions carefully. At times he would partially come out of his depression and be stronger emotionally, but then I would forget to be careful.

I knew how much he hated the snow and cold. Since he wasn't adequately dressed, I didn't expect him to stay out long. Besides, this was the night before Thanksgiving and one of our daughters had arrived home from college only minutes before.

We were planning a special welcome-back-home supper.

But Jim didn't return in time to eat with the family. We have a strong family tradition about waiting for everyone to gather before we eat, but each of the girls had other, previously arranged commitments, so they finally nibbled on something and went their separate ways. This kind of situation had never occurred before in our family. The special meal and I waited. I reset the table for two with special placemats and candles.

Eventually Jim did come home. He accepted my apology and seemed amiable as we ate our meal together by candlelight. Little did I know how much anger toward me was still raging within him, but most of all, he couldn't understand his confusion and the terror from his deep internal struggles.

We went to bed, and he spent the night in a furious battle that I didn't know about until morning. I didn't know at the time how close we were to that being the last night we would be together in our bed.[1]

IT SHOULDN'T HAPPEN TO HIM!
At the time Jim was the senior pastor of a large church. He has faithfully preached and lived God's Word for over 25 years. Literally thousands of people benefited from his wise counsel. God had given to him gifts of empathy, wisdom, insight, peacemaking, creativity – and the list could go on.

He is a thorough thinker and has learned to apply Scripture relevantly to daily living. His education has included 2 master's degrees and 2 doctorates from highly respected Universities. His undergraduate work and his graduate programs have included much psychology, as well as theology. As a young man Jim had set goals for his life which frankly, I thought were beyond what he could ever attain. But by his early 40s he had met all of those goals, plus some exciting experiences besides.

We had 3 daughters, young women who were maturing in the Lord, and we were proud. We always had to be careful financially, but we lived in a nice house, thanks to early parental help, and Jim's building and remodeling abilities. Our family had a great number of physical illnesses and injuries through the years, but we found these to be opportunities to grow and trust God. We were basically a happy and well-adjusted Christian family.

CRUMPLED LEADER

Then our strong leader with the optimistic outlook on life and "edgy" faith in the Lord began to wavier. He became depressed and grumpy. He began to doubt God's goodness and love. The messages he preached were still strong, but he told me privately that he felt like a hypocrite. He frequently had a compelling urge to run away. At first we thought he was simply overworked, so his desire to escape was natural. But the restlessness in him came from something deeper. He didn't understand much of it, but he did recognize it as the same phenomenon he had watched in other men at this age.

He began to see the whole world in general – and our marriage in particular – as awful. He would declare, "Everything stinks!" Then he would try to bully me with philosophical questions such as, "Why did God make us in the first place? Why do we have to live this life?" He seemed obsessed with wanting to be young and enjoy things he felt he had missed in his life of sacrificial

Christian service. He often questioned the values by which he had lived. Of course, this was threatening to me since our lives were so entwined.

YOURS TOO?

My husband's midlife crisis has a happy ending. But perhaps your husband is just beginning the midlife trauma. Or perhaps he's in the middle of his crisis and you're not sure there ever will be an end – let alone a happy ending. Maybe you've noticed that other midlife husbands were having problems – but never thought it would happen to your guy.

Or perhaps you weren't even aware of the turmoil in other midlife men until you realized something was wrong with your husband. However your awareness came, now as you sense that your husband may be on the edge of midlife disaster, you are afraid – afraid for him, and afraid for yourself.

The man you married, who has all the fine abilities and qualities, is changing. You want to tell him you appreciate him, but how can you when he is so hard to live with? You don't like his changes. Grouchiness and angry words often replace his customary kindness and gentleness. Restlessness and vacillation erode his usual stable composure.

Instead of exuding an air of confidence and boldness, he often seems anxious and insecure. Sometimes he wants to be babied – at other times he demands to be left alone. He is aloof and doesn't talk, or he lashes out irrationally at everyone and everything. He wears an air of martyrdom.

Before he was optimistic and challenged by difficult

problems, now he now sits depressed and immobilized by self-pity. He sometimes lets obligations slip by without meeting them as he did faithfully for years. He has trouble at work, avoids his old friends, and finds excuses for not spending time with you or the children – plus he shuns social activities at every opportunity. Perhaps he has resigned his leadership positions in the church, or has given up coaching soccer. And sometimes he is so profane in his complaints against God, that you wonder, "Who is this man?"

These changes in your midlife husband are symptomatic of a struggle going on deep within your guy. He is battling with very profound and basic life questions. Some of his questioning may be traumatic for you and for him – but the process is necessary.

If your husband is in his 40s, his midlife transition is taking him from the competitive, goal-centered, hard-driving days of his 30s into a more relaxed, more people-centered period of his 50s. These may be anxious, confusing days for both of you, but if your husband successfully integrates the conflicts raging within him, there will be better days ahead. In fact, your marriage relationship will probably be more satisfying, his attitude toward his occupation or profession will improve, and he will be a better man in many ways.

WIN OR LOSE

As the wife of a husband who is experiencing a midlife crisis, you need to know some basic facts. You can help him through this difficult time. Whether he blows it or grows through it, may depend a great deal on your response. We will look at the problem from your husband's perspective, and from yours. Then we will examine what resources will help you to be strong, and what you can do to help your husband during his midlife crisis.

But you have to decide to dig in and do the necessary work. Perhaps you've been through so much that you are too discouraged to even try. Maybe you don't believe there is such a thing as a midlife crisis, or you're not convinced you need to get involved. Once you've considered the evidence about midlife crisis in men, and learned how to cope personally, then you'll want to work at being part of the solution.

During Jim's crisis I learned that a determination to grit my teeth, bear the burden, turn the other cheek, and fill the air with positive thinking wasn't enough to carry me through the long, hard days – and nights. God's grace was also essential. More than ever I needed a good relationship with God, who promised to be with me wherever I went and – *whatever I went through.*

I want to encourage you to take Isaiah 43:2-3 as your own special verses,

Do not be afraid, for I have ransomed you. I have called you by name; you are mine. When you go through deep waters and great trouble, I will be with you.

When you go through rivers of difficulty, you will not drown!
[Wow! God, I'm glad you promised that, the waters seem to be closing over my head right now.]

When you walk through the fire of oppression, you will not be burned up; the flames will not consume you. For I am the Lord, your God – your Savior.

Now let's look at the facts about a man's Midlife Crisis.

2

THEY NEVER WARNED ME!

A lot of time, effort, and money has been spent studying certain phases of life – childhood, adolescence, the senior years, and even women's menopause. But until recently there has been little acknowledgment that there are other stages in adult life. Thankfully, starting in the 1960s researchers such as Daniel J. Levinson,[1] Bernice L. Neugarten[2] and Roger L. Gould[3] have observed and accumulated massive data on adult developmental life stages. There is documented proof that adults do go through several transition times, and one of the most painful is "Midlife."

THE GAP

For years we have recognized that women experience varying degrees of stress during menopause. In fact, most libraries have a number of books on the subject – but have you checked the shelves for books about men at midlife? There are a few, but not many offer help or hope, and some border on the porno with lurid tales of the sexual escapades of midlife men.

Many physicians, psychologists, and psychiatrists have been

slow to admit that men go through a midlife trauma. Perhaps it's because most of the professionals are men – and men must be strong, stable, and invincible. That's the conditioning of our society. Perhaps medical doctors and counselors have been too busy with the "urgent needs of patients" to reflect on the accumulated data about the symptoms of their midlife male patients and their wives. At least the door is now open, and doctors and therapists are acknowledging the results of research and their own observations.

NEW AWAKENING

Christians have also been silent on the subject. There wasn't much written about midlife men from a *Christian* perspective until Jim's book, *Men in Midlife Crisis* [4] came along. If you've not read Jim's book, we suggest that you do. It will tell you what a man goes through, and give you a good understanding for what we'll be sharing in this follow-up book.

For a long time Christians thought that any midlife man who began behaving in strange and sometimes un-Christian ways had a spiritual defect or deliberately turned away from God. Religious people talked behind their backs so they "could pray more intelligently for them." Midlife men were shunned and frequently confronted with "straighten up or get out of our group!"

Some Christians are quick to grab the ammunition of 1 Corinthians 5, showing the need for purity in the church, but they are slow to act on Galatians 6, which teaches us to help stumbling people back onto the path – not kick them while they are down! That same chapter also warns us to remember that we might be the next ones needing help.

Some of us find it easier to stand upright and kick a fallen brother out of the way, than to bend down – dirty our knees – and help him get up again. But Jesus commands us to share each other's troubles and problems. And the midlife crisis is a problem! The New Living Translation paraphrases Galatians 6:3 in this way, "If anyone thinks he is too great to stoop to this, he is fooling himself. He is really a nobody."

Watch Jesus caring for troubled and sinful people – it's a picture of understanding, kindness, and gentle guidance. But He was harsh and direct with the rigid, follow-the-letter-of-the-law, religious people. Jesus took time to understand people's problems and share their hurts. When we take the time to get into another's shoes, we are a lot less critical – and we begin to feel the pain of the midlife person.

MIDLIFE MOUNTAINS

More Christian counselors are now aware that men go through a real struggle during their midlife transition. I (Jim) wrote in my book *Men in Midlife Crisis*, "It is a time when a man reaches the peak of a mountain range. He looks back over where he has come from and forward to what lies ahead. He also looks at himself and asks, 'Now that I've climbed the mountain, am I any different for it? Do I feel fulfilled? Have I achieved what I wanted to achieve?'"[5]

"How the man evaluates his past accomplishments, hopes, and dreams will determine whether his life ahead will be an exhilarating challenge or simply a demoralizing distance that must be drearily traversed."[6] In either case, he is in a time of trauma, as never before, because his emotions are intensely involved.

The middle years need to be understood as years of change and loss. As men age from one life stage (young adult) to another (midlife), they must adapt to their changing needs of self-esteem, meaning, identity, and quality relationships. What used to satisfy young men won't work for midlife men – they feel grief, pressure and anxiety as they grope for workable solutions. Our national research shows about 70 percent of men experience a moderate to severe crisis, with anxiety, or inappropriate behavior.[7] Other men enter this transition with quiet desperation, not as painful – but still debilitating.

Sally and I have learned from talking to hundreds of men and women that many men everywhere experience a traumatic time at midlife. The stories men and their wives tell us are often heart-shredding, yet these stories nearly always follow very predictable patterns.

John, our personal friend, was a kind, loving husband and father. He was a spiritual leader in church. He worked overtime to provide for his family. Some time ago he began behaving strangely. He became irritable and depressed. He spent money the family didn't have to buy clothes and a sports car. He seemed obsessed with trying to look young.

His wife said, "He insists on taking a vacation without me. Now I've learned that he is living with another woman. He claims our marriage hasn't been any good for years, and it's entirely my fault. He is angry and unreasonable with our children and says we are all just parasites living off him."

THE TIP OF THE ICEBERG

Some research shows that as many as 80 percent of American men suffer moderate to severe symptoms during midlife, while other studies report almost 100 percent.[8] By the year 2000 the largest U.S. population group had shifted from youth to midlife. The number of adults between 35 and 45 increased 75 percent, while the number of youth increased only 5 percent." These numbers tell us that a massive number of midlife men and their wives are undergoing midlife stress at the same time.

Because of the secrecy and ignorance surrounding many of the real concerns of midlife men, men and their families have often suffered alone. They have felt their internal struggles and external events were peculiar to them – not realizing they were part of a normal developmental pattern. Tangible research evidence is mounting that the midlife crisis is a common occurrence.

WHEN DOES IT HIT?

Our work with midlife people, as well as other research, indicates that the midlife crisis range may occur as early as 35 and as late as 55. Sometimes an external event, such as the loss of a parent or friend or a drastic change in job status, forces a man into an open battle with the internal evaluation that is going on. Sometimes, however, the tragedy causes him to suppress questions until later.

THE URGENCY OF "NOW"

As men age and enter midlife, they benefit from hindsight. When men were in their 20s, they pushed confidently ahead, easily taking career risks. But when they reach their 40s, they want to recapture what they feel they have missed. In their 20s, men behaved with seeming invulnerability and timelessness, but in their 40s, they give way to fear – a terror that time is running out.

Another problem for many midlife men is they don't know who they are. A man may have lived all these years not assessing who he is and not exercising his individuality.

In the first years of a man's adult life, men set aside self-assessment and self-definition. Instead they yield to the expectations of mentors, wives, and bosses. Their role as father, husband, provider and employee defines them. They don't really know who they are, just what they do for others. Later, this "auto-pilot" behavior changes into a desire to rebel. It is the revolt of the midlife man.

After a man gives the basics to those dependent on him, he realizes what he has missed – a sports car, a sail boat, time off for recreation, etc. These rebellious displays are symbols of inner frustration – a growing sense of depersonalization and demasculinization.

During twenty years of counseling people, Sally and I began to recognize the midlife stress as a common phenomenon. Wives usually were the first ones who came to us about marriage problems, but occasionally men came for help. We eventually noticed that the behaviors and stresses of the men around age forty fell into a similar pattern.

Then I (Jim) experienced my own midlife crisis! During that time we were both doing research to write my book *Men in Midlife Crisis*. After some agonizing months, I reached a breaking point in my experience and God gave me assurance that I was going to make it with my life intact. The manuscript for my book was finished, became a best seller, with help for men and their wives. (More than 1 million are in print in several languages.)

"THAT'S MY HUSBAND!"

As soon as our book, *Men in Midlife Crisis* reached bookshelves, we were further convinced that the male midlife crisis was indeed a fact – and that it was rampant all over the United States. Telephone calls and letters came from hundreds of women telling us the book had described their husbands to a "T"! When we spoke on radio, television, or at conferences, both men and women, Christians and unbelievers, overwhelmingly identified with the crisis.

Just after *Men in Midlife Crisis* was released, we developed a multimedia presentation to visualize the midlife situation as we spoke at meetings. I took hundreds of pictures of midlife men on beaches, in physical fitness centers, in sports car salesrooms, in offices, at construction sites, and other places. Each time as I asked permission to take pictures, I explained why I wanted these pictures – to picture "Midlife Crisis." Many of these men acknowledged that they were also right there. Many were surprised and relieved to know that other men also experienced the problem.

We think these verses may give you hope during this midlife time.

> **Unless the Lord had helped me, I would soon have died. I cried out, 'I'm slipping!' and your unfailing love, O Lord, supported me. When**

doubts filled my mind, your comfort gave me renewed hope and cheer. (Psalms 94:17-19)

There really is an upheaval at midlife, now we need to ask, "Why it is so traumatic and unsettling?"

3
WHY SO MUCH AT ONE TIME?

Why can't midlife be a time of quiet evaluation of looking at the past, setting new goals for the future – and just enjoying the process of living? Why must men go through so much introspection and exhibit weird behaviors? When husbands, who have been generally stable, dependable, and optimistic, suddenly change – wives are especially bewildered. Something has hit their husbands – and they are afraid the change is permanent.

Levinson notes that because midlife men are often somewhat irrational, others may regard them as "sick," but what they are going through is normal. (That doesn't mean it isn't painful, but it is normal.) He "is working on normal midlife tasks," according to Levinson, and "the desire to question and modify his life stems from the most healthy part of the self."[1]

At first I (Sally) found it hard to understand why Jim needed to analyze every aspect of his life when he was in his mid-forties. Often I didn't realize everything he was evaluating, but when he let me know, it was strange that he couldn't simply accept life as it was. As he shared more about his struggles with aging and the meaning of life, I began to see that he was rethinking his whole life. And often he wanted to be alone to do it.

A "MOLDY OLDY"

A forty-something man notices his body changing, and he may have experienced the peak of career success, plus he is acutely aware that he is not young. He can do some things to keep his body in shape and to improve his physical appearance and endurance, but he cannot stop the aging process. He cannot deny the gradual physical decline – hair color, hair loss, failing eyesight, reflexes, muscle tone, and that dreadful weight shift. All these changes are the inevitable downhill slide toward old age and DEATH!

By forty he feels he may feel has gone as far as he will go in his occupation, or he doesn't have much time left to get to the top. He may not be pleased with his attainments, or even worse he is beginning to realize that he may never reach his dreams. If he has met all of his goals, he still could be unhappy – especially if he wanted more. A man's self-worth is massively tied to his work and his ability to keep pushing and creating. Our culture values youth and productivity, but his midlife wisdom, insight, and an easier approach to his profession usually is not appreciated. He can be replaced, and that's frightening to his self-esteem, and his financial future.

Prior to forty he was considered a part of the younger generation – with energy and creative ideas, but now he is looked at as part of an "older generation." Twenty-something people do not regard him as a "peer" but, as "dad" rather than "buddy."

His role with his aging parents is probably reversing, and

he is now becoming their nurturer. He may need to assist them financially, and he may need to help them in emotional ways by spending more time with them and guiding them in the decisions they face. It shocks him that in too short a time he will be the senior citizen needing nurturing from his children.

Betty shared with us how her pastor-husband, Ralph, had thought he'd finally feel good when he got old enough to be respected for his wisdom and experience. By the time he was in his 40s he was senior pastor of a church with three younger staff. Ralph envisioned them all working together as a team, but two of them were immature and Ralph had to hover over them to see that their share of the ministry got done. The third was very independent and had no desire to blend his work with the others. In fact, he began to work behind Ralph's back to gather a group to eventually overthrow Ralph.

This all happened at a time when Ralph's father was dying of cancer and their last child had gone away to college. Betty could see that Ralph was grieving more over the absence of their son than over the impending loss of his father. Sometimes he secretly resented his father's need for attention while he was so consumed with trying to hold the church together – and keep his job. Betty also felt very anxious about the church situation and missed their son.

Fortunately, Betty took time to let Ralph talk about his problems and fears, and he was eventually strong enough to work with his circumstances. As a result, one staff person moved on, another grew up, and Ralph accepted a larger church position.

LIFE WITH HIS WIFE

A man's marriage may be the biggest source of his unrest. Each mate has been busy succeeding in their career, paying the bills, serving the community, and raising the children – they didn't even notice that their relationship had stagnated. Now as he questions everything, and wrestles about continuing the same routine, suddenly his marriage seems unsatisfying and downright miserable. Affairs, divorces, and remarriages are common during midlife, as some men decide the commitments they made in their early 20s are no longer valid – or satisfying.

Irritants and disagreements which existed all along, but were ignored, now become festering sores. Because a man often doesn't understand the reason for his restlessness and depression, he finds it easy to blame his wife. He begins to feel that the marriage has always been rotten – "It was a mistake to get married in the first place!" He exaggerates the negatives because he sees all of life as a giant unfulfilling disappointment.

Most wives are unprepared for this blame and rejection – and besides she has a list of her own complaints. Since she doesn't understand her husband's midlife transition, she doesn't know it is only temporary. She often aggravates the situation with her own poor reactions and decisions. Yes, it's natural and understandable for her to want to meet her own needs, but her understandable self-centeredness at this time will only worsen the situation.

One day we received an agonizing phone call from Carol after her husband, Gary, had left her. Through her tears she explained that they had been having stormy times during the last few months. Gary, who owned an appliance store, had become unusually restless and angry with Carol, and the children. Then he had started coming home late from work. When she demanded explanations, he exploded. She was afraid he was having an affair.

Finally one night she accused him of being late because he was seeing another woman. He exploded, "If I am, it's none of your business. But it was her business, and she kept after him to tell her one way or another. He refused to answer and went off to watch TV. This confirmed her suspicions. Alone in the bedroom she sobbed in despair – and prayed.

Finally, she decided to have it out with him. She charged into the family room, punched off the TV, and demanded that they have an honest talk. Gary ordered her to turn the TV back on and leave him alone – he had nothing to say to her. Carol lost her temper and began screaming at him about taking time for everyone else but her. He became furious, slammed out of the house, and was gone until very late.

Several more such episodes occurred, sometimes because of her suspicions about another woman, sometimes because he wasn't taking care of things around the house, or he was threatening to sell the business. Finally during a fight one night, he left and didn't return.

Carol was convinced he had become impossible and their marriage was over, so she filed for a divorce which was to be finalized in a month. Then she read our book *Men in Midlife Crisis,* and began to understand that it was exactly what her husband was going through and then realized she had handled things improperly. What could she do now? That's when she contacted us, and we began the helping process – they began to understand each other, and eventually they restored their marriage to a "better than ever" state.

TOPSY-TURVY

To a man in his 40s, life is like a pile of important papers tossed into the air during a windstorm. As they scatter all over the yard, he scrambles to catch them before they blow out of sight. The chase makes him tired, dizzy, and discouraged. Plus now he has to sort and reorganize the papers deciding if some should be discarded, or if missing papers should be rewritten. And it certainly would help if his wife and everyone else weren't standing there, nagging and pressuring him while he tries to put the pieces back together!

Every aspect of the midlife man comes into question. This profound reappraisal cannot be a cool, intellectual process. It will involve emotional turmoil, despair, the sense of not knowing where to turn – plus feeling stagnant. Many men going through this stress make several false starts. He tentatively tests a variety of new choices, in the middle of his midlife confusion. Sometimes he will act irresponsible or impulsive. He feels a need to explore, to see what is possible, to perhaps fantasize about a new love relationship, or a different occupation, or to just run away. Every genuine midlife reappraisal will be agonizing, because it challenges his beliefs from his young adult era – plus he wrestles with all of the pressures of his current life. That's why we call it a **Midlife Crisis**.

When a man is evaluating the existing structures of his life and deciding which parts to keep, modify, or discard, he experiences so much turmoil that it often shows in his behavior

– grumpiness, anger, depression, withdrawal and frequent times of hiding in his lonely cave of self-pity.

CHRISTIANS ARE SUSCEPTIBLE, TOO

"But if he is a committed Christian, won't he avoid all that?" many ask. I (Jim) often reply, "That's like telling a ten-year-old boy he can avoid his teen years by becoming a Christian!" A teen must go through the teen development years – it is crucial for normal progression to Young Adulthood.

We recognize adolescence as a normal developmental stage. Every teenager has certain emotional tasks to accomplish to become a healthy, mature adult. Psychologists and sociologists now recognize the midlife transition as a normal stage of development. Have you noticed how similar the symptoms of midlife and adolescence are? That's because the people involved have similar evaluation processes to complete. The major difference is that midlife men carry a lot more responsibilities, have more people depending on them, are decreasing in physical vigor, and are losing society's respect for their age.

A teenager who has made a personal commitment to Christ will certainly go through the teen years of testing and deciding life's values more easily. But that doesn't keep him from having to go through adolescence. Likewise, being a committed Christian is a definite advantage for the midlife man, but it doesn't prevent him from experiencing the normal developmental transition time, nor is he absolved from working through the necessary tasks of this stage of life.

EXCESS BAGGAGE

How smoothly the midlife transition is made depends upon

many factors, such as emotional baggage from earlier years, whether he made wise occupation choices in line with his talents and abilities, and whether his marriage is satisfying and growing. Feigenbaum, who has conducted studies with upper-middle-class men, found that the *severity* of a man's midlife crisis was also influenced by birth order (the firstborn shows more severe symptoms), plus the wife's perception of the problem, and whether or not the man is in a power struggle with his children.[2]

Sally and I feel that a man's midlife struggle may be less severe if he has worked through the adolescent and young adult issues. 1. "Autonomy", the ability to stand on your own without being obnoxious. 2. "Interdependence", the ability to work as a team with other people, and 3, "Intimacy", learning to give and receive love. Working through these issues will give both teens and their Dad confidence and understanding for what their gifts are and who they are.

Dave was forty-one when he went into severe depression and rebellion. He and Anita had been married 21 years. They were both young when they married, after Dave's second year of college. He was the older of 2 sons and had lived with his parents to save money while going to college. He also helped with the family's small insurance business. His younger brother had gone away to college.

During his third year of school and first year of marriage, Dave dropped out of college to work because Anita was expecting their first child and had to quit her job. Dave intended to go back to school as soon as they got on their feet financially, but babies and medical bills continued to come. He finally gave up the hope of getting a college degree and continued to work in the insurance office where he originally thought he'd only be temporarily. He received promotions through the years and the pay was good, but he had planned to be a civil engineer and never felt contented in the insurance business.

In her late 30s Anita decided to go back to work. She also decided to take night classes at the junior college, so she would be eligible for a better position with her company. Their four children were still at home and often were left on their own. Two of the teens began having trouble in school and the oldest started hanging around with a tough bunch of kids.

Dave decided it was time to crack down, but he didn't get far. His teenagers were belligerent and disrespectful. Anita was gone much of the time and she was tired and not involved when home. He began to resent her freedom and lack of interest in him. He also felt it was time for his brother to help care for their elderly parents, but the burden still fell mostly on him.

After years of hassling with his children, heavy responsibilities for his parents, and disinterest on the part of his wife, Dave was coming apart. He finally called us for help. We worked with him for several months before he began to heal and resolve some of his intense struggles with his brother, parents, teens, and his wife.

Dave said he would not have made it without God's help.

> **Lord, you alone are my hope. I've trusted you, O Lord, from childhood. Yes, you have been with me from birth; from my mother's womb you have cared for me. No wonder I am always praising you! (Psalms 71:5-6)**

In this chapter we have begun to understand a little bit about a man's midlife crisis, but what about a woman's crisis, and what if they both have crises at the same time? A woman has some distinctive problems of her own at midlife. In the next chapter we will look at some of the woman's midlife issues – which may increase the marriage stress.

4

BUT WHO CARES ABOUT ME?

Women go through a series of developmental stages, too. If your husband is going through his own midlife crisis, hopefully you are also not in your midlife crisis. If you are not in a crisis, you are in a better position to help him. And, hopefully, during your midlife stress times, he will be strong enough to help you. You truly need each other.

BALANCING THE SYSTEM

William Lederer and Dr. Don Jackson in *The Mirages of Marriage* support a premise Jim and I have found true in our marriage. A marriage works on a "systems" concept. The whole is more than the sum of its parts. The whole is made up of all the parts, plus the manner in which the parts operate in relation to each other.

Lederer and Jackson point out:

According to the systems concept, a change occurs when related parts are rearranged. The closer the association, the more obvious is the action-reaction. If an influence upsets the balance, then a compensating factor must be provided by the system to regain balance.

Marriage is not just a relationship between two rigid individuals. Marriage is a fluid relationship between two spouses and their two individual systems of behavior. The totality of marriage is determined by how the spouses operate (behave) in relation to each other. In physics it is accepted that for every action there is an equal reaction. The same law holds in psychology and in human relationships.[1]

A balance has to be maintained in a marriage relationship. If you are sick and need care, your husband's response should be one of nurturing and helping during your illness. If he is not well, you must find extra strength to care for him. We have found that many midlife women possess a great deal of strength and endurance to cope with the situations created by their husband's midlife crisis. Many women never thought they had such strength.[2]

MID-THIRTIES TRAUMA

Some of a midlife woman's strength may come from the fact that she has recently weathered her own midlife reevaluation time. Many women experience an unsettling time in the last half of their 30s see our book *Women in Midlife Crisis*.[3] Age is catching up with them, usually a little sooner than for their husbands. Their children are off to school all day and need her less. If a woman chooses a career outside the home, she may feel threatened by younger, sharper women, and she may wonder if she should have followed a more intensive career path. Husbands are often so engrossed in their careers that they have little time for their wife.

Midlife women begin to question their worth, their choices, and their values. Gail Sheehy calls it "the crossroads for women."[4]

Some decide that now is their last chance to make life different. Thirty-five is the most common age of the runaway wife. In the mid 1950s, there were about 600 runaway husbands for each runaway wife. Currently, the average is about one runaway wife for each runaway husband.

Sometimes her midlife crisis strikes very suddenly – some event often is the final straw which breaks her midlife back. For example, she may have been wondering why her husband is no longer interested in her – or that her teenage children are acting like teenagers – disconnecting from her. She may be having employment problems because her skills are out of date – or she may feel that no one in her world really wants her.

Then she steps out of the shower and looks at her body in the full-length mirror – suddenly she is confronted with her aging body. Everything seems to have "gone south." What happened to all of my youthful firmness? And when did I pick up these saddlebags? I always made jokes about my college friends who were overweight – but now I'm the one who is overweight!

Suddenly she feels alone, unwanted, out of control, and she may wonder if her life has any purpose. This may start her into a deep process of questioning her values and the directions she has chosen for life – she is now in a full "midlife crisis".

The positive result is that she will refocus her energies for the future, probably pick up some new skills, and she will learn to relate to her children, parents, and her husband with a new mature depth which would not have been possible without going through her own midlife crisis.

Jim and I have written a full length book on the stress and confusion of women at midlife, plus we share how to make this time positive. The book is titled, *Women in Midlife Crisis,* and is available at some bookstores, or on our website www.midlife.com.

MENOPAUSAL MISERIES

Midlife also has a second blessing for women, "Menopause." Menopause generally begins near the end of the 40s or in the early 50s. Hopefully, your husband will have safely traveled through his midlife crisis by this time and he will have developed into a mellow, sensitive, and loving person – which many studies predict.

Some women go through their menopausal years with little difficulty. Others suffer a great deal physically and emotionally. Some physicians say a woman's emotional troubles, during this time, come from how she handles external circumstances and problems, and are not caused by menopause itself. Other medical doctors and counselors, however, feel that nutrition and hormonal balance affect emotional stability during this time and a woman cannot simply "will" herself to be strong.

> **Save me, O God, for the floodwaters are up to my neck. Deeper and deeper I sink into the mire; I can't find a foothold to stand on. I am in deep water and the floods overwhelm me. I am exhausted from crying for help; my throat is parched and dry. My eyes are swollen with weeping, waiting for my God to help me. (Psalms 69:1-3)**
> **The humble will see their God at work and be glad. But all who seek God's help lived in joy. For the Lord hears the cries of his one; he does**

not despise his people who are oppressed. (Psalms 69:32-33)

Both the late 30s evaluation time and the menopausal process of the late 40s are crucial times in a woman's life. Now let's look into detail at the wife's problems, while her husband is in his midlife crisis.

Part two
YOUR DILEMMA

5

LIFE OF A MIDLIFE WIFE

A husband's midlife crisis will cause a wife some of the greatest stresses she has ever experienced. She will be shocked to see her husband begin to question values and choices she thought had been settled long ago. She will have trouble understanding why he is so concerned about his aging. When he accuses her of being the cause of his problems, or he gives her the cold, silent treatment, she will feel rejected, misunderstood, and perhaps very angry.

The reality of her husband being attracted to younger women will cause her terrible anxiety, because she knows she doesn't have the body she once had, even if she has been careful about diet and exercise. But, after all, she bore his children, sat up nights with them, now chauffeurs them, administers their activities, and has been doing double duty with them, the house, and perhaps a job besides, for all these years. Of course, she has crow's-feet at the corners of her eyes and her hair may be graying! She wishes he could accept her aging – and his.

If he is having trouble at work, or has even quit, there will be financial strain. His self-esteem has probably taken a beating, so he will take out his frustrations on his wife and kids. When he is grouchy and irritable, his wife may try to cover for him with family and friends. She will make excuses when he withdraws and refuses to be involved. If she babies him, he will want her to leave him alone; if she ignores him, he will want her attention.

In such a situation, a wife will find herself on the horns of a dilemma. She may try to help her husband see the world more correctly, but he seems to be wearing the wrong glasses, and they certainly aren't rose-colored! She may feel as if she is tiptoeing around dog poop all the time. One misstep and you've slipped and fallen in the awful mess!!

WHO ARE YOU?

If you think about life without your husband, you will probably be frightened. After all, your life has revolved around him and the kids. You wonder how the family will manage financially. The kids' lives would be ripped apart without him, and that would intensify your misery. You're back to where you started in your wrestling with your present situation. Life with him is sheer agony – but life without him could be worse.

Several women's books blast some midlife women for having settled for only being a wife and a mother. It's true that at this time in life, her children hardly need her, her husband may be dissatisfied with her, or take her for granted. Women's books and magazines often say she is losing all she has lived for – her life has been a waste. But it can be equally as tragic for a woman to be only involved in a career outside the home and find her career to be her *only* identity.

If it is wrong to be *only* Mrs. John Smith, or the mother of Bobby Smith, is it not just as sad to be *only* a personnel manager, television producer, or vice-president in charge of production? I (Sally) have had careers both in my home and outside, and I didn't find the outside one to be any more satisfying – and certainly it was not as rewarding as the inside one.

Your identity needs to be drawn from the quality of person you are, wherever you spend your energy. True, you are known by what you do, but you *should be* known by your "being," while you are "doing." You need to be flexible and realize that your roles may change. Whether you are a wife, mother, or employee, you are still the same person, and you have a mission in life.

A woman with Christ in control of every aspect of her life has an advantage. She has an identity in Him. (See 1 John 3:1-2 and Ephesians 1:6.) She also has God's Word and His Spirit within her to cause her to mature. (See such exciting verses as 2 Peter 1:34; Galatians 5:22, and Philippians 1:6.) The capstone verse for me is, ". . . we Christians actually do have within us a portion of the very thoughts and mind of Christ" (1 Corinthians 2:16b). That ought to make a difference!

Let's face it, though, your husband's midlife crisis will make you reevaluate your identity. What he decides to do with his life affects yours. Who will you be if he changes jobs, or quits work entirely? Who are you if he has an affair, or divorces you?

FEELING SHREDDED

Tied closely to your identity is your emotional life. Actually, all are closely knit – your emotions, spiritual life, physical being, social person, and so on. A woman cannot be divided into isolated segments. Each part of you affects the others. Your emotions, however, will probably take their worst beating during your husband's trauma.

Sally and I have asked women across the United States to respond to several questionnaires about life during their husbands' midlife crisis. Following are some of the emotions women felt as a result of their husband's midlife behavior. Women reported that they felt:

- Insecure
- Anxious
- Rejected
- Confused
- Afraid
- Fearful to be alone at night
- Hateful

- Jealous
- Worthless
- Angry at God
- Unloved
- Lonely
- Naggy and pushy
- Withdrawn
- Desirous of escape

You could probably add more to the list. Some of the emotions Sally felt couldn't be identified, but she said, "I experienced very definite physical symptoms from my emotions. It was like being in the spin cycle of the washing machine and then run over by the wheels of a freight train. It was like an icy slushy which gives you those stabbing pains in your brain, and stomach. One minute I would be hopeful – the next I was back to feeling anxious and afraid. Each new development brought another set of feelings to face."

ON OR OFF WITH GOD

In questionnaires we asked women about their spiritual lives during their husband's midlife crisis. Some drew closer to

God, while others felt more distant and angry at Him. Some continued attending church services and Bible studies, others quit because of embarrassment over their situation, or because of the way church members treated them. Some spent a lot of time in prayer, others couldn't pray. Some said they learned to genuinely accept Christ's forgiveness and help and felt less judgmental of others.

Those who turned to God with their problem felt He had been faithful in strengthening them and helping them to personally change – even if their prayers for their husbands were not answered in the manner they wanted, or as soon as they hoped. Those who studied their Bibles and claimed its promises felt that the struggle had been worth it because of the spiritual maturity and closer fellowship with God they experienced.

MISFIT WITH SOCIETY

A husband's midlife crisis cannot help but affect the wife's connections with other people. She often will cover up for him and make excuses for his behavior. She may find herself dodging certain topics of conversation, or hedging on answers to "friends" and "relatives" questions. Some women feel they have no true friends at this time, and they feel very lonely. Other women, however, accept their friends support and encouragement.

Our chat rooms have been a powerful resource to connect, and encourage women whose husbands struggle with midlife crisis. To connect with our chat rooms, go to our Internet address – www.midlife.com.

Often a woman either has to stay at home, or she goes to social functions alone. If she goes alone, she is considered the "odd duck" in the group. If her husband has left her, she feels she doesn't fit in social situations, or sometimes is not even invited. If she is divorced, other women may feel she is a threat and they don't want her around their husbands. Sadly some men think the woman with midlife marriage problems is fair game for their advances.

MISUSED AND ABUSED

A wife also suffers physically. The tension makes her tired. Sometimes her fatigue is so great she would collapse under ordinary circumstances, but she feels she must keep going so things don't get worse. She often doesn't get enough sleep because of worry, waiting for her husband to come home, or the dread of a long late-night argument. She may overeat, or not eat enough of the right foods. Ulcers, acne, menstrual complications, headaches, heart trouble, and other symptoms may be some of the stresses her body experiences.

Some women are physically abused by their husbands during this time. Some men become angry, and so frustrated that they have beaten their wives – even those who have previously been gentle. In fact, spousal abuse is becoming a serious national problem. Because women are trying to shield their husbands, protect the family reputation, or because they feel they deserve it, they often do not report the beating or get help for themselves.

SEXUAL STRESS

A wife's sexual life is probably altered during this time. Some midlife men experience impotence, though most cases prove to be psychological rather than physical. There is a natural decline in male sexual ability by midlife, but if accepted as normal the change can be sexually positive rather than negative. His speed at reaching orgasm may be slower and the frequency of his orgasms may be less, but his effectiveness as a satisfying lover can be greater. Some men are threatened as the wife becomes more sexually aggressive and emancipated – a documented phenomenon for women at this age. If a man is experiencing sexual problems, he should see his doctor who may prescribe a sex drive enhancing prescription, such as Viagra.

Sarah and Frank had experienced a strange turn of events in their sex life as they neared their twenty-fifth anniversary. Sarah began to initiate sex, something she had never done before. She bought seductive clothing and tried various other enticements. Instead of responding positively, Frank felt threatened and was cold and disinterested. Sometimes his withdrawn attitude dampened Sarah's spirits so she went to sleep frustrated. A few times her sexual advances won out, but most often Frank wined that he just didn't have any sexual feelings anymore.

Even if a husband's sexual functioning and desires are nearly the same as before in pre-midlife crisis days, a wife's tension over other aspects of his behavior may inhibit her emotions for a satisfying sexual relationship. If her husband is having an affair, his sexual ability may be hindered because of his guilt, and you can believe that if he is having an affair and she knows it – her sexual response to him will be altered!

THE FINANCIAL CRUNCH

When we asked women how their financial situation was during their husband's crisis, many replied that it was difficult, especially if the husband had left home and was paying for his own apartment. Finances are also drained if the husband indulges in toys such as a sports car or another expensive item he has previously denied himself – or especially if he spends money on the "other woman."

Some men, according to the answers on the questionnaires, were still providing as usual for their families, a few were even more generous, but some men were doing less because they were spending more money on themselves, on affairs, or due to a job change. Some families lost benefits such as health and life insurance if the husband had quit his job. Under some company policies, divorcees lose all benefits. Many women report that housing and money are less important – they are more concerned about rebuilding the relationship with the husband.

Midlife is potentially a very painful time, which seems to have more questions and problems than answers.

> **Be still in the presence of the Lord, and wait patiently for him to act. Don't worry about evil people who prosper or fret about their wicked schemes.**
> **The steps of the godly are directed by the Lord. He delights in every detail of their lives. (Psalms 37:5-6, 23)**

We have thought a little about some of the things that happen to a midlife woman personally during her husband's crisis. Now let's think about the midlife woman's marriage relationship.

6

LIFE WITH A MIDLIFE MAN

Even though a couple may have experienced a fairly stable marriage, the midlife crisis will surely test it. If there have been unresolved problems before the crisis, they will now be magnified. A poor marriage will probably get worse – and may not stand the strain.

Bill and Helen are a typical example. They were married 20 years ago, when Bill was quite emotionally immature. Helen was very confident and began making most of the decisions for the family. Bill didn't notice, because he usually didn't recognize that decisions had to be made. Helen also had very definite opinions about how Bill should do things, including his work – and she was always sure to pass on her insights to him. Unfortunately she often did this in the form of criticism, ridicule, and nagging.

Eventually Bill, the mild-mannered consultant, came to resent her domineering ways, but he did not have the courage to confront her about it. As her bossiness became more oppressive to him, he escaped by taking a job that required lots of travel away from home. Gradually they grew apart – and didn't even know each other interests. Helen had to manage the family while Bill was away, so she continued running the household even when he was home.

As Bill entered his 40s, he began to realize that life was slipping by, his children were growing up and soon would leave home – and he didn't know his kids or his wife anymore. He began to long for intimacy with his family. Yet, when he spent more time at home, Helen made him feel as if he no longer belonged and she picked at him incessantly. He didn't like being on the road, but he couldn't stand being at home either.

THE ONLY WAY IS OUT

When Bill told Helen he wanted a divorce, they finally sought a counselor. Helen was shocked because she felt they had a good marriage. When the counselor met with them, he noticed that Helen dominated the session. When the counselor asked her if she understood some of her husband's needs, she quickly and strongly said, "Of course." The counselor noticed Bill wince.

It soon became apparent that Helen knew little about Bill's needs, or his personality, his views, his values – or any aspect of his life. Sadly, she didn't even know that she didn't know. Bill did not know how to express himself or set boundaries about her domineering ways. His solution was to escape.

With the counselor's help, they each began to see their own part in the situation. They decided they were willing to work on the problems. As Helen backed off with her bossiness and Bill began to communicate his thoughts and feelings, their relationship improved rapidly. They started taking time to understand each other and to meet each other's needs. Soon they found they had fallen in love again.

Of course, they still had to keep working at their weak spots, because people don't instantaneously break long-term poor lifestyle patterns. However, they were both Christians and relied on God's power to help them change. Now that they had tasted the joy of a better marriage, they had the necessary motivation to keep working at it. And they are still married.

LOW TIDE

By the midlife years, marriage is usually at its lowest ebb in satisfaction. Young couples start married life feeling close, spending time together, doing things to please each other, enjoying their sexual experiences, and expecting continued bliss.

As they each get busy with their own careers and the children, it is harder to find time to communicate and keep up with each other's daily lives. Answering the demands of other urgent matters robs them of the intimacy which earlier had drawn them together. The less they know each other, the easier it is to drift even further apart.

When midlife crisis hits, a man needs the help of a strong marriage – yet he is least likely to have it during the toughest times. A guy may feel that his wife doesn't realize, or even care, that he is struggling. He finds it hard to let her know. Their communication is only about the business of running the family. They no longer exchange ideas or talk about their feelings. Their sexual relationship may be almost nonexistent because they are always tired and busy. They find their married life to be dull and boring, boring, boring. And any strife between them makes them both miserable.

THE BALL AND CHAIN

Often midlife husbands feel trapped by responsibilities and want to escape from pressure. He looks for the cause of his pain and finds it easy to blame his wife. He is tired of working hard to keep up with the heavy expenses and everyone's demands on him for his time, energy, and decisions. Since his emotions aren't as stable as they were previously, he is apt to look back over the years of his marriage and remember only the bad times.

Because he is weighing his life values, he is probably questioning whether choices and commitments he made 15 or 25 years ago are going to fit his future. The conclusion might cause him to consider changing his marital commitment. "Besides," he thinks, "this woman is getting old and she reminds me that I'm also getting old. I feel lots of energy when I'm around younger women."

Women, you are in competition! It isn't a fair competition, but you are competing! You are being judged according to the youthfulness of your body, your face, your interests, energy, and your playfulness. There's no way you can win using those standards. You have to compete and win in other ways. Later we will talk about how to win this tough competition.

Because you are busy with your own concerns, you may resent the time your husband needs during his crisis. Your communication may be so poor that you have no idea what he is going through, and you don't want to spend the time to find out. Or you may feel he can be ordered to "snap out of it" – the rest is up to him.

Perhaps he was never the leader he should have been, and you've had to take over. Now he is complaining that you are too bossy. Or he may have led in the past, but now he says he can't. Sometimes he wants you to make decisions. Other times he resents it if you do.

NOW WHERE?

The whole course of your marriage for the present and the future seems uncharted, and the maps you've been following seem to be faulty. You may feel like a little girl lost on an unfamiliar path in the woods at night. What do you do now? The roles you each have been living now need reevaluation. Your family situation has changed, and so have you.

Surely there must be some absolutes to follow! Thankfully there are. And now is the time to do some careful searching of the Bible about husband-and-wife relationships. Do some thoughtful thinking about your personalities, history together, your life-style, and your total family experience. Sometimes we quickly decide on "pat" guidelines and force our mates to follow them whether or not they are really right for our family.

God gets the credit (or blame) for a lot of fast, three-step fixes for marriage relationship problems that really are man-made (or woman-made), or have come down from a long line of traditions that have their beginnings in pagan culture. For instance, much of how we look at husband and wife roles in marriage comes from ancient Jewish tradition which was influenced, not by God's commands and principles, but by the surrounding pagan world.

Marriage roles continue to be distorted by those who promote the dominant male – subordinate female theory, or those who advocate female manipulation of men. One extreme is as bad as the other. An unbiased look at the meaning of the original language of the Bible on these subjects is an eye-opener – see books such as those listed in the Chapter Notes.[1]

During this transition time for you and your husband, you can do some careful weighing of Scripture, study good Christian books, and listen to the counsel of godly people in deciding God's way of living out the nitty-gritty details of your marriage. The information from these good sources might be conflicting and still leave you baffled, but God promises to give you wisdom, if you ask for it. I've found that if I stop worrying about what to do in a particular situation, quiet down for a minute, and ask God for his wisdom, he really does give it! ". . . He is always ready to give a bountiful supply of wisdom to all who ask him. . . ." (James 1:5).

WEIGHING THE WAY

How can I tell if the thoughts that come to me are God's wisdom and not my own thoughts, imaginations, and desires? James 3:17 gives us some guidelines to determine if the insights we receive are from the God or not. Any insight, or course of action I feel led to take, must line up with the following paraphrased concepts. "But the wisdom that comes from heaven is first of all pure and full of quiet gentleness. Then it is peace-loving and courteous. It allows discussion and is willing to yield to others; it is full of mercy and good deeds. It is wholehearted and straightforward and sincere."

God's wisdom is untainted by my selfishness, past grievances, suspicions, or unrealistic hopes that my husband is going to do what I want him to do. True wisdom is also quietly gentle, loves peace, and is considerate. A lot of so-called insight from the Lord would fail at this very point of being courteous. Spiritual wisdom has room for discussion and hearing the other point of view. It is even willing to yield to the other one! Godly wisdom is compassionate and follows up with an understanding of your mate's pain with action and attitudes to remove or reduce the problems.

SINCERELY WRONG

God's wisdom is also enthusiastically candid and straightforward. Perhaps the ability to be direct or specific about a subject is the one criterion of wisdom that is the easiest for us to use – and misuse. We often misinterpret frankness as the sure sign of wisdom when, in fact, being outspoken must be carefully balanced with all the other facets of wisdom.

True wisdom is also sincere. Sincerity by itself cannot be a test of wisdom, because we can be sincerely wrong. That's why we need the balance of courtesy and listening to the other's point of view.

It is easy to make some bold and sincere decisions that we think is God's leading – when we consider only our side of a situation. Allowing discussion and being willing to yield to others is a more appropriate way to ensure God's wisdom in decisions. True spiritual wisdom can stand the strain of listening to another person's point of view. If I am too threatened to hear my mate's view, then I need to reevaluate my source of wisdom.

Allowing for discussion means that you need time to communicate. Busyness may cause you not to know your mate's thoughts and feelings well enough to understand, or to meet needs. Perhaps you have lost a great deal of emotional intimacy and may not even realize it.

HIS NEED FOR INTIMACY

Becky was a hot, sexy blonde who caused men's heads to turn for a second or third look. Bill, a "hunk" and a university student, told me he couldn't stop thinking about her. He sheepishly confessed that he constantly dreamed about touching Becky's sexy body. Their dates were passionate times of exploration – followed by the sad process of confessing to God that they were sorry that they had again slipped into sex. You see, Bill and Becky had promised themselves, and God, that they would focus on building a holy relationship, one that would match their call to be missionaries.

Soon they were seeing me regularly for practical counsel about how to enjoy the truth that they were sexually magnetized by each other – yet able to restrain themselves, so they could focus on developing other aspects of their relationship. They were continually facing the shame of pre-marital sex which did not match their life calling of being missionaries.

After a year of learning to live with their sexual tensions, and developing other aspects of their relationship, I had the joy of marrying them. Soon they entered Grad school to prepare for missionary work – all seemed ecstatically wonderful beyond belief.

After they had spent fifteen years in ministry and raised four children, their passionate love life started to cool sharply – so much so that Becky told me she was repulsed if she rolled over in bed and bumped into Bill's body. She explained that he was 100 pounds overweight and didn't seem passionate about her any more. Before they were married, they had to struggle to not touch each other.

Soon the sad story started to unfold – too busy, too stressed, and different hobbies and interests. Then Bill suddenly joined a gym and started losing weight, wearing his hair differently, and was frequently gone, without any explanations to offer.

Then Becky discovered all the signs – Bill's coolness, notes in his clothes, mysterious cell phone calls, and email. It then became clear that there was another woman – "Now what do I do?"

If intimacy is gone, or not missed, it doesn't mean it isn't needed. Each individual has a set of needs, whether or not he acknowledges them. He either consciously or unconsciously does what is necessary to meet those needs. A man may need someone to listen to him, to help him think through the areas he is wrestling with, or to encourage him to go through his reevaluation process. If you're not communicating, you may not recognize his needs and – he may think you don't care or wouldn't understand.

However, there may be another woman available who does seem to understand and care. If a man begins to spend time sharing with her, he may find himself involved in an affair, which he never intended. Previously he might have avoided becoming entangled with another woman – but at midlife he is very vulnerable because of his confusion, frustration, and dissatisfaction with every aspect of his life. His inner confusion may push him over the edge.

The situation may be complicated by him blaming you for all of his problems. He may feel you are the cause of his entrapment in work which he hates, that you don't care about him, or you are nothing but a nagging mother to him. Right or wrong, he may make many accusations against you. Probably he will not tell you what he feels, and in reality, he isn't even aware of his own feelings. Some midlife men feel justified in pulling away from their wives or vomiting anger on her – because, in his perception, she is the total cause of his unhappiness.

> **The Lord says, 'I will rescue those who love me. I will protect those who trust in my name. When they call on me, I will answer; I will be with them in trouble. I will rescue them and honor them. (Psalms 91:14-15)**

In the next chapter, we'll look at the difficult question, "How does a wife handle the situation if her husband becomes involved in an affair?"

7

LIFE IN A TRIANGLE

Generally, a midlife man does not deliberately set out to have an affair. The other woman is most often a person he already knows, and with whom he has natural contact. He is attracted to her because she seems to care for him and understand him. Often she is considerably younger, because at midlife he is avoiding people his own age who remind him that he is getting old. He likes to be with people who have youthful attitudes and ways of thinking.

YOUNG IS GOOD

He is attracted to younger women whose bodies are still in shape and whose faces are not lined and weary – then he can forget his own wrinkles and bulging stomach.

This doesn't seem fair to his wife, because there is little she can do to change her physical aging. Growing old is simply the natural result of living life – which they both have been doing. After all, his body isn't the same "hunk" it once was either. His face is also wrinkled, and his hair is getting gray and thin. He is in the denial stage regarding his aging, and he doesn't want to accept his own deterioration. Being with someone younger gives him an adrenaline rush – and that feels good.

CAREFREE INTERLUDE
Because many pressures are converging upon the midlife man, he consciously or unconsciously seeks relief. One way is by finding some carefree activity he can enjoy. Another woman may provide a fun experience without responsibility – like a day at Disneyland. She doesn't discuss the household or family with him. She doesn't come to him with the problems of the broken washer, a son's trouble in school, or the high dentist bill and she also doesn't point out his neglect or critical attitude. The "other woman" hasn't had to put up with his inability to make family decisions, crabbing that your mother visits too often, or failing to keep his promises to attend your daughter's piano recital. He only presents his best side to her.

He probably has shared with the "other woman" every miserable part of his life – his rotten deal at work, his rebellious kids, and his unhappy relationship with his wife. He hasn't said things to belittle the other woman nor cause her personal anxiety, and she is very focused on being the sympathetic listener to his woes. In so doing, she keeps his attention – plus *she is pathetically needy,* and craves his attention.

Another woman can provide some lighthearted breaks in a man's dreary, heavy world – at least initially. She doesn't have to share his responsibilities, and she is free to do "fun" activities with him. The excitement of getting to know a new person can be exhilarating and adventurous. The mystery of the unknown is often scintillating – and can be a welcome contrast to the rest of his life. He is drawn more and more deeply into the affair, if only to experience relief from his oppressive burdens – real or unreal.

TIME TO SERVE HIMSELF

Many men have been living sacrificial lives for 15 or 20 years. They have willingly accepted an increasing number of commitments at work, in the community, at church, – and with their growing family. By the time a man reaches midlife, he is becoming physically exhausted, and emotionally drained. He dreams of relief, but then he is tied to obligations he cannot graciously escape – even for a little while. He feels trapped by the commitments he readily accepted as a younger man. But now they are heavy, oppressive burdens. He begins to get sick and tired of it all. His need to escape becomes compulsive. He thinks, "I'm tired of serving other people! It's my turn!" Having an affair is his attempt to serve himself.

Let me state emphatically! We are not giving excuses or permission for affairs! We are only stating the reasons people get hooked into affairs. If you are really going to understand your husband, you also need to understand the confusion he experiences which leads to an affair. Understanding the affair does not mean that you approve!

Henry was a Christian who had denied himself recreation all of his life. For years he had put in double time in his profession, mostly to provide good things for his family. He suddenly took up golf and spent every moment on the golf course. He worked much less and was away from home even more than before. His wife complained, but said she didn't care to join him when he once grudgingly suggested she come along. Before long Henry met a divorcee who liked to golf, and their time together on the golf course led to an affair.

TOTTERING VALUE SYSTEM

Midlife men are evaluating what is important in life, and they are doing it when their emotions are depleted. Their value system gets a thorough shaking. They're not sure their moral standards have been right. They may think it was unnecessary to have been so rigid. They may question biblical principles, even wondering if a God-consciousness is still important. Temporarily they are confused and need to do *tons* of sorting of their values. But take hope, the moral God-code within them, a code they have been taking for granted for years, will help them through this difficult time.

When your husband is walking on this unstable ground, he needs understanding and empathy. If you are preoccupied with your life issues, or you yell at him to "straighten up," he is a likely candidate to look for someone else's caring. If that someone else is a woman, a relationship may get started which ends up with complications for all of you. Quoting Scripture verses about what is right and wrong is not the kind of help he will accept at this time. Scripture is not given to us as a weapon to club someone. It is given for our growth. Now is the time to learn from the Bible about the best way to help your husband.

GROWING APART

Many midlife couples divorce because they have grown apart. They simply don't have anything in common. Their interests are widely divergent. As we have said, this separation usually happens because the couple has not spent the necessary time together to keep their love strong. They each have been busy succeeding in their careers – either in or out of the home. If those careers do not cross paths, they become distant as they develop their specialties. An obvious remedy for this growing separation is to spend lots of time keeping up-to-date with your ideas and feelings.

Sometimes one mate participates in a class or activity which brings about a new self-awareness or self-development. If the other partner isn't involved in the activity, he may feel left out. It may not be possible for both to participate, but the participating partner should share their experiences with their mate. Ideally, both mates should be growing, and they should be communicating about their growth.

We know of several couples who experienced serious conflict because one spouse was outgrowing the other. Bob and Karen are a classic example. After several years of raising children, Karen started a small business that brought her into contact with many interesting people. About the same time, she began attending a weekly women's Bible study and started growing dramatically in her spiritual life. Before long she was using her business contacts as a means of sharing her faith. This led to times when Karen counseled troubled people. She found fulfillment in helping others. She soon felt the need to get counseling training, so she took an evening class.

Soon the tension exploded between Karen and Bob. He was aggravated because of the amount of time she was giving to her business and her classes. If any housework was neglected, he pounced on her. Karen felt Bob was becoming narrow and stuffy, but when she suggested he take advantage of growth opportunities. He snapped, "I'm too busy making a living – somebody in our family has to work!" He felt her business wasn't much help to the family income, and he also felt that she was getting too high and mighty and looking down on him.

Instead of appreciating the new ways she was expanding as a person, Bob felt threatened and put down by her. Karen found it easier to share her spiritual insights and growth with close friends instead of Bob. Some of these friends also took time to have fun together. Because Bob didn't know them well, he said he was too busy to join them. Karen often left Bob at home and went out with her friends for these social times.

Fighting between Karen and Bob increased. Bob was unwilling to understand or support Karen in her growth, and he felt no need to do any growing. Karen felt Bob was a shriveled, visionless person, and she was unwilling to give up the new fulfillment she had recently found. Sadly, their marriage ended in divorce.

POSSESS ME NOT

Some midlife men enjoy being with other women partly to prove their wives don't own them. The wife's possessiveness doesn't enhance their marriage – and it may destroy it. A vicious cycle sets in – the more you clutch, the more your husband resists. The more your husband resists, the more insecure you feel and the more you clutch. A man's personhood is stifled when he feels possessed, and he may become angry. The anger can take many forms – perhaps even an affair.

One of the greatest gifts of love is to give your husband the freedom to be himself. Granting freedom doesn't mean you condone immorality, but it does mean you recognize that he must make his own life choices. Giving your husband freedom doesn't mean you are indifferent or cold. It means you acknowledge his right to be a person. When you try to dominate his thoughts, actions, and will, you are setting yourself up as

God – but, you are not God. If you free him, it doesn't mean he will automatically abuse the freedom. So, don't let your "clutchiness" drive your husband away.

TROUBLE AT WORK

Sally and I had a good marriage – we were generally doing all the right things, but as the pressures of the responsibilities of a Senior Pastor of a large church increased exponentionaly, I became a "grizzly bear" to live with. From my point of view, everyone was incompetent and no one was getting things done right – or on time! Of course nothing was wrong with me – it was all them!!

Think about your husband's job stress. Job satisfaction and how a man likes himself are closely linked. Often a man cannot control what is happening with his job, so he takes his frustration out on his family. By criticizing his wife and children, he is attempting to gain control of part of his life.

If you are an encourager about the job stress, you will strengthen your marriage as you work together against a common enemy. Sadly many husbands battle work problems alone. The hostility toward his wife may not only be because of work stress, but because the wife doesn't understand his stress. This hostility can grow into open warfare.

Many factors contribute to a midlife affair other than a husband's wanton lust. The reasons he strays do not excuse the affair, but understanding the causes might help you do your part ahead of time, so that an affair doesn't happen.

But suppose an affair is already taking place. How do you

handle it? What feelings will you have, and how will you respond to them?

PAIN FOR YOU

Painful and debilitating emotions result from a husband's affair – hurt, humiliation, rage, rejection, retaliation, and indescribable loneliness. The hurt a wife feels is not only because a younger woman might be involved, but because any other woman is involved. A third party has been allowed to share what was intended for only you two. The affair hurts more than any physical wound and will need resolution and healing.

A wife will also likely feel anger, confusion, and self-pity. She may feel rejected, and her self-image may hit zero because she feels worthless. She probably cannot understand any reason why her husband should do such a thing. She may become defensive and say she did not contribute to the affair, or she may become overly self-blaming and tear herself apart with unreal guilt.

The emotional stages, when a wife learns of her husband's unfaithfulness, usually are denial, reluctant acceptance, then anxiety, grief, anger, and finally a determination to stay in – or get out of the marriage. The stages are similar to stages with other tragedies in life or death. Each stage needs to be adequately dealt with in order to reach peace at the end. To think that we can skip one stage, or suppress it, is a mistake. That particular emotion will surface again and usually returns in a more complicated, dangerous form. Allow yourself to feel each emotion – it's painful, but necessary.

Donnas' husband asked her for a divorce. Unknown to her,

he and his secretary had been having an affair for years. Finally he told her, and he said he intended to marry his secretary. Donna refused to believe him and would not believe any of her friends and relatives who verified the affair. She denied the situation so long, without moving into the other necessary stages, that when her husband completely moved out of the house and began living with the other woman, she nearly went insane.

She had always been an emotionally strong woman and a committed Christian, but her behavior became bizarre and she tried unsuccessfully to end her life. When she finally allowed herself to grieve and feel angry, she was able to begin to make realistic plans for her future and her children.

EMOTIONS ARE NOT IMMORAL

Emotions such as anger, anxiety, and grief are normal and not wrong in themselves. How you react because of the emotions, however, may be wrong. But you don't need to feel guilty because you have these feelings. Many Christians have carried a lot of irrational guilt for years because of the emotions they experience. Accepting the fact that emotions are not sinful, has been liberating for Sally and me. What I do as a result of my emotions is another matter!

Think about how you handle your anger. "Constructive" anger generates the desire and energy to do something helpful about the problem. "Destructive" anger causes harmful effects, such as depression, cruel words, and hurtful actions – often regretted later – and almost always complicating the original problem.

The hurt and anger a wife feels over her husband's affair,

and another woman, are reasonable emotions. How she handles her emotions will play a part in her husband's response. If she explodes and lowers the boom on him, she will probably drive him away. If she suppresses her feelings and tries to cover her true reactions, those emotions will later erupt in some worse form, such as severe depression, attempted suicide, irrational behavior unrelated to the real cause, or even a serious physical illness. If she assumes an uncaring attitude, as protection for herself, her husband will feel she doesn't care about him.

WHERE DO YOU GO FROM HERE?

If you learn, or suspect, that your husband is having an affair, you need to be honest with yourself and with your husband. Acknowledge your feelings, but control them. Don't suppress or stifle them, but don't let them rage out of hand either.

Perhaps the best advice when you first learn of your husband's affair is to do nothing – take a deep breath, and invite God into the situation. Don't act too quickly. Instead, reflect on your marriage. Evaluate the meaning of the affair – to him as well as yourself.

Don't go into hysteria or deliver hasty ultimatums. Keep calm and work toward opening up communication with your husband.

We have found that a wife with an unfaithful husband must make some basic decisions. If you don't face these basic questions at the beginning, then you will be pushed around by everyone else's opinion about what you should do. To help you answer these key questions, start by listening to God, and your heart.

If you decide to stay in the marriage, don't try to get him to confess the adultery through questioning, innuendo or other forms of entrapment. Tell him straight out that you know about the affair, and how you know. But wait until the first shock is over before you talk about it. When it's time to bring up the subject, don't use threats, such as divorce or separation, and don't keep reminding him that you feel betrayed, and that he has forever lost your trust.

GAMES WIVES PLAY

You must not play games. When your emotions are topsy-turvy, game playing may be your automatic response. You may feel you need to make your husband pay for what he is doing to you. Your actions and the atmosphere you create will then take on all sorts of vengeful expressions. Or you may feel so sorry for yourself that your tone of voice and mannerisms will drip with misery.

Marian decided she was going to make Ted, her husband, pay for leaving her and living in an apartment while he tried to sort things out. He came home frequently to be with her and the children, and they sometimes had sex while he was home – but he would always leave without staying overnight.

She decided she was making things too easy for him by allowing him to have both the intimacy of family life, and the privacy of his own apartment. She hastily decided to take the children and move out of state, so they wouldn't be so convenient for Ted. They are now legally separated, and Ted is spending evenings and weekends with another woman and her children.

Marian had really hoped Ted would beg her not to move, and

come home permanently. But Marian gambled – and lost. Many men do return home to stay, and marriages become stronger than ever. But usually there is a wife who is patient, and waits for him to be ready to come back – plus she does her own growing and changing. But Marian's game went too far.

Kay, a reclusive artist, was the epitome of weakness and self-pity when her husband started his midlife crisis. He never left her, but we marveled that he didn't. Kay's voice whined. Her shoulders drooped as she dragged around the house, barely able to keep functioning. She let her appearance go, no longer bothering to use makeup and seldom washed her hair. Her husband was unusually moody and withdrawn during this time, but Kay didn't try to find out why, or volunteer to help him. She was too consumed with how he was treating her.

He took longer than usual making his midlife transition, and neither of them grew much because of the experience. The problem was that both of them were focused on their own needs, not on trying to understand or to meet the other's needs.

You might take the tough, "I'll-make-it-no-matter-what" stance, and your very being bristles with grit and determination as you wear your "I-could-care-less" armor. Or you may be the completely defenseless martyr sighing, "That's what I get in return for all I've given him, but I'm still willing to die for him." Games don't help – they cloud the real issue – so stop playing games and become truly genuine.

WHY DID IT HAPPEN?

Ask yourself, "Why did my husband get into the affair. What were his needs? What attracted him to the 'other woman' and what should I do now to solve this sickening situation?" Speak and act in gentle ways – don't use strong-arm tactics. Your goal is to restore your marriage, not get revenge or prove how unjustly you've been hurt. But it is so hard not to want to get even and strike back when you have been hurt so much.

Wives are often surprised to learn that an affair doesn't happen because the husband is looking for better sex. He may be looking for attention! Assure your husband that you want to learn what his needs are and how to meet them. (But don't be shocked if he can't tell you his needs – he likely is so confused that he really doesn't know himself. Remember, most men don't understand feelings, nor do they know how to share. He really isn't trying to fool you – he just doesn't understand himself.)

If he is in distress over his job, let him know that you will stick with him through any decision he must make. If he trusts you, he may use you as a sounding board to think through steps to change his work situation. And if he is seeking your help, Jump For Joy!!

UNDERSTANDING IS CRUCIAL

We know that most men have trouble expressing their feelings, and if your husband feels unhappy about his work, he may be afraid to admit it. He feels a heavy responsibility not to fail – and to provide for his family. Most men have trouble with "living up" to the expectations of others, and most men lack the courage to change – fear generally holds them prisoner. A wife who understands this struggle potentially is the greatest help for her guy's personal growth.

Understanding your husband's problems and his feelings

is one of the best keys to rebuilding your relationship. Since my (Jim's) midlife crisis, I've often said that Sally was my best friend during that time. Sally was the one I talked to when I felt like talking. I could tell Sally the very worst – and I knew she would stick by me.

You may need to develop a new awareness of your husband's desires, reactions, and attitudes. It takes practice, practice, practice – and don't give up when you blow it, just start again. It helps me (Sally) to think of "tuning in," much the same as finding a channel on the TV. The station is broadcasting all the time, but I don't see it until I turn on the TV and choose the correct channel.

You can tune in to your husband by asking nonthreatening questions, then genuinely listening to all he has to say. Remember to be empathetic, show tenderness, and encourage him – all with an attitude of respect. Be sensitive to your timing. Don't force him to start your "discussion session" on your schedule – "Sit down right now even if you are late for work!" Be ready when he is relaxed, open and the circumstances are right.

WHO ELSE CAN HELP?
You may want to see a marriage counselor, but it is likely your husband will not. Most men do not want to admit they need help, because it makes them feel as if they have failed. Perhaps he will agree to go at least once in order to help you with your needs. If you find a counselor who understands the midlife situation, and who develops a rapport with your husband, your husband may decide to continue marriage counseling. But don't be surprised if he doesn't. Usually counseling doesn't work until later when a husband decides he is ready to work on restoring

the marriage.

There are many good marriage books available, and some of our suggestions are in the Suggested Reading List at the end of this book. Sally and I have written 15 books – several of which deal with midlife issues. You might consider together reading some of our other books such as, *Traits of a Lasting Marriage, Men in Midlife Crisis, Women in Midlife Crisis, Pure Pleasure,* and *When a Mate Wants Out.*

Our close friends Bill and Pam Farrel[1] have written over 40 powerful books about marriage and family, plus issues facing both men and women. The Farrel books are lots of fun to read. Some of their best selling books are, *Men Are Waffles, Women Are Spaghetti, The Marriage Code,* and *Red Hot Monogamy.* Bill and Pam offer great insights as well as fun do-it-yourself activities to strengthen your marriage. To learn more about Bill and Pam Farrel's ministries visit www.farrelcommunications.com.

A Christian woman who wants to restore her marriage must draw upon the resources available in Christ. And you will need them all! It is so easy to let your humanness get in the way, or take control. Being well acquainted with your Bible, and drawing on the strength of its promises, will be one of your biggest assets. There were times when I (Sally) felt as if all I could do was hang onto the hem of the Jesus' robe! (Luke 8:43) I constantly needed to ask for the God's help to prevent game playing, wrong motives, self-pity, and a host of other negatives which wanted to take up residence in me. I needed to go to God continually for a correct perspective on our midlife crisis problem.

SPECIAL FRIENDS

Having a human friend helps – a real friend with whom you can share your problems will be vital in your ability to cope. You must be sure, however, that you don't simply use the friend as a dumping ground for all of your husband's faults. The friendship should be one in which you find strength to go on while you are in this desert. Acceptance by another human being enables you to know you are still worthwhile. The friendship, however, should not take away from the time that you should be spending with your husband.

A wounded wife needs an outlet, but some women spend so much time and energy "talking out" their problems, that they create new ones. They may neglect their job and family, or they may give too many personal details, and damage their husband's reputation so it is nearly impossible for him to return to his former life. Dwelling only on negatives will make chances of restoration very slim. Your friendships should encourage you to grow and change, and also help you to keep an objective view of your situation.

You should be sure that your intimate friendship is with women – not another man. You need special support and affirmation, but you may mistake male affirmation for love. Because of the vacuum in your relationship with your husband, you can easily fall prey to the attentions of another man – even though he may have initially intended only to help you. Your husband's affair probably happened because of a vacuum he was feeling in his relationship with you. Since you so desperately need security at this disruptive time, you must not look for it from another man – or you may also become involved in an affair.

If you are part of a small group of caring Christians, you probably can find safe support from them. Small Bible study groups, or other groups, are likely to be alert to the needs of their members, and able to offer genuine love and caring.

Our chat rooms also give the opportunity to connect anonymously with people who are experiencing the same struggles as you. Some of these people have had their marriages restored. They will be a great source of insight, prayer support, and encouragement. Our chat rooms can be found on the internet at the address of www.midlife.com.

KEY RESOLUTIONS

A matter that must be totally settled is forgiveness. Before you can expect to see any change in your husband's actions or attitudes, you must decide whether or not you will forgive him for his unfaithfulness.

Later we'll share more on forgiveness, but for now adopt the attitude of Colossians 3:13, "Be gentle and forbearing with one another and, if one has a difference [a grievance or complaint] against another, readily pardoning each other; even as the Lord has freely forgiven you, so must you also [forgive]" (Amplified Version). If you know Jesus Christ as your Savior, you have experienced God's forgiveness. Because God has forgiven you, you are enabled to forgive your husband.

We know several marriages that have been preserved mainly because a wounded wife has been willing to forgive her husband. We also know couples who could have resumed a good marriage after an unfaithful husband repented, and he was willing to work on the relationship – but for various reasons his wife could not forgive.

It is true that infidelity and desertion are scriptural grounds for divorce, but generally everyone in the family profits more from a restored marriage than a broken one. Remember, you are not forced to get a divorce, just because you have scriptural grounds.

If you have decided to work to save your marriage, draw on God's strength and wisdom to control your emotions, to totally forgive your husband, and commit yourself to be patient during this process. Your husband may or may not be ready to work on the restoration of his marriage, and even if he is willing, changes will not happen overnight. It takes time, and pain, to bring about the birth of a baby. Sometimes the development of a better marriage relationship is as long and laborious – and rewarding – as the emergence of a new life.

> **Happy are people of integrity who follow the law of the Lord. Happy are those who obey his decrees and search for him with all their hearts. They do not compromise with evil, and they walk only in his paths.**
> **I will obey your principles. Please don't give up on me!** (Psalm 119:1-3, 8)

You may be saying, "Well, that's fine for other women, but it's too late for me – my husband has completely left me! What do I do now?" Read on – there is hope!

8

LIFE WITHOUT HIM

The Midlife era has the second highest divorce rate of any time in married life. (The very highest rate is during the first year of marriage.[1]) In addition to divorce, there are also a great number of Midlife marriages which are broken by abandonment. The cause is usually a mate's attempt to get relief from the tremendous pressures at this time in his life.

If your husband has left you, you are probably going through one of the greatest trials of your life. You are probably experiencing the emotions of – rejection, hurt, anger, failure, and guilt – the same as the woman whose husband is having an affair. Your husband may not have left you for another woman, but he is gone nevertheless.

ESCAPE THE PRESSURE

Many Midlife men leave home because they don't know what else to do to relieve their tensions. They want to be alone to sort things out. They want to be free from the constant family demands they face when they are in the home. They don't feel like meeting anyone's needs – but when they are at home they feel guilty about not meeting the needs of the family. They want peace and time by themselves without constantly feeling guilty.

Some men leave home because they think leaving will be best for the family. They feel so messed up and confused that they think it would help the family if they just got out. Some men actually believe they are going crazy and their family would be better off without them. What they don't realize is that their leaving causes more pain, than if they stay.

However some midlife men are actually driven out by their families. Their wives and children demand that they leave. In those cases, the wife is not open to considering her part in the family stress – she thinks the husband is the one who needs to change.

FIT FOR THE GARBAGE HEAP

We have heard many true midlife stories, but one of the most memorable was told to us by a man who really thought he must be going crazy because of his strange feelings and frequent uncontrollable behavior. One night as he was eating dinner at home with his family, the sheriff arrived at his door with divorce papers and documents ordering him out of the house within one hour. His family was sitting right there – they had never discussed this with him. They had decided he was crazy and, without talking with him, they made arrangements to expel him.

The man was stunned! He gathered up some of his possessions and left. Convinced he really was insane and worthless, he decided to end his life. He drove to a pawnshop and bought a handgun. The owner had to show him how to use it. He decided to drive to the city dump to shoot himself. He felt good-for-nothing. He thought the dump was a suitable place to leave his body. But when he arrived, the dump was closed and the gate locked.

By now he was very distraught, but he knew of another dump which might be open. As he got back out on the highway, he was speeding and driving so erratically that a patrolman stopped him. The officer didn't notice the loaded gun on the seat beside him, but gave him a ticket for speeding.

Somehow that intervention of another person was enough to snap the frantic man back into reality. He began to realize he didn't really want to kill himself and decided, "Hey, I can't be all that bad. Maybe I'm not as crazy as my family thinks I am." His perspective began to return and he started working on his problems. Sadly, his family did not take him back, and his wife divorced him. He has tried to live as happy a life as possible, but now as an old man he feels he missed out on many of the good times he could have had with his children in their adult years.

Other men have told us their wives have laughed at them for breaking down and crying over their confusion about "who they are," "work problems," and many other difficult issues which they are wrestling with during midlife. After relentless berating or scoffing from their wives, many men can't see any other alternative, but to leave.

YOUR STRUGGLES
Whatever has caused your husband to leave – problems at work, your persistent nagging, his own inner turmoil, or his desire to live with another woman – you and your children will face problems without him in the home.

The anxiety of what the future holds is one of the greatest stresses. It is hard to trust the Lord with something so unpredictable as the result of your husband's absence. Your fear is that he may never return, even though he might tell you his leaving is only temporary. As agonizing as this time is, it helps if you can keep looking at the "big picture." This time is only part of the whole. Many men do return. And if the couple has done some growing and changing, the marriage can be stronger than ever.

Al, the accountant, and his wife Janet now have a strong marriage which is meaningful for both of them, but their relationship was on shaky ground during the worst time of Al's midlife crisis. Al moved out for several months, and although he was never involved with another woman, he did get involved in computer pornography. Janet often felt anxious about what would happen, but she decided the best way to help Al return would be to give him her loving understanding and concern.

Sally and I became her confidantes and encouragers during this time. We urged her to understand Al's needs and try to meet them. She knew one of his needs was more time for relaxation. Al wanted her with him during his recreation times, so she resigned from a volunteer position in the church to be with him. He also wanted her to share responsibility in the accounting business he was building as a second income. So Janet took an adult education course in bookkeeping. When Al saw that she cared enough to make some adjustments for him, he soon came back home and was willing to work with her on rebuilding their marriage.

TIME TO GROW

Many women we know work on self-improvement while their husbands are gone. They start physical fitness programs, computer classes, real estate courses, or go to college to finish their degree. Many women have found books – printed or e-books, podcasts, CDs, small groups, plus our chat rooms at www.midlife.com to be helpful as they worked at the issues which bothered their husbands – such as nagging and weight. Often husbands find their wives more attractive because they are growing and changing. Even if a husband isn't impressed, or doesn't return home – a woman is a better, more fulfilled individual for having grown.

"But," you remind us, "I have my daily life to struggle through. I feel stressed every waking minute. How can I carry on a somewhat normal life?"

That is where your dependence upon God comes in. He promises to be with you everywhere – all the time. He is there to be leaned upon. He knows your heartache and bewilderment, and he wants you to pour out your heart to him because he promises to be your refuge.[2] He also wants to guide you step by step, and God offers you his wisdom as he promises in James 1:5, "If any of you lacks wisdom, he should ask God, who gives generously to all without finding fault, and it will be given to him."

Angie is one woman who has relied on God to help her while her husband has been living in his own apartment. She often feels tremendous hurt, but she has also found that God is a healer. Many times she has shared with us the new things God is showing her which help her to understand her husband's problems and assure her of God's love. Sometimes she is hit with a new disappointment, but she has learned to turn each situation over to God and ask Him to lead her.

Your self-image has taken a hit because you felt rejected when your husband left. You probably feel worthless. You may feel you are a failure in everything, including your marriage. You need to get your eyes off your troubles and look for what is still good.

When I (Sally) get depressed, as I turn my eyes away from my problems, Jesus gives me a balanced perspective once again. Take time to remember the good things about yourself and who you are because of God's grace. The little book, *31 Days of Praise,*[2] by Ruth Myers, will daily help to focus you away from the dreadfulness of your problems, and give you a new perspective – it's a great book![3]

I (Jim), find that listening to praise music gives me a new focus. I also find that stepping outside of the office for a few minutes and letting the sun beat on my face, helps to change my perspective.

Do things which help you to feel good about yourself – get a fresh hairdo, have lunch with the girls, work on your favorite hobby, take a class at your local community college, or do some voluntary service in your community. If you like to read, give yourself permission to take time to read. Make time to be with friends so that you get input from sources other than your own mind. Blocking out time for your own stability is not a luxury – it's survival!

MORE HASSLES

If your children are living at home, you have their needs to consider too. It is difficult to be both father and mother, especially when you are a hurting mother. As hard as it may be, you must give your children quality time. They really need your support. The man who left is *still their father*. Connecting with your children is so important that we have devoted the entire next chapter to the subject.

If your husband is not continuing to support the family as he did before he left, finances will be one of your major problems. If you were not working outside the home, you may need a job now. Finding a suitable job could be a big hassle and the process may also be hard on your self-image. If you quit a career to get married or care for your children, you may find that younger women are handling your job with more skill than you now possess. You may find it difficult to get work hours which are convenient for your family, and you may find sexual discrimination in hiring and wages.

Lois, a brilliant young woman, was awarded a four-year scholarship to attend a university – but gave it up to marry Ken. She had been more than willing to give herself to being a wife and mother. Five children and nineteen years later she found herself divorced – with inadequate child support. She was forced to go to work, but she no longer had marketable skills to earn what she needed. She was forced to take a job at minimum wage, be on her feet several hours a day, and work evenings and weekends – when she should have been home with her children. She not only had the heartache of divorce, but Lois had to cope with a very different life-style, unbearable fatigue, and neglected kids.

Relating to friends, neighbors, and relatives at this time may also be difficult because you feel embarrassed and uncertain. Be honest with these people. Think carefully about what you're going to say – don't be a bitter "husband basher." A small group can give you perspective during this difficult time.

It is better if the news of your husband's exit doesn't travel to too many people immediately. Your husband will be able to come back more easily if fewer people know, and the people who do know, should know very little. If your husband wants to return, he will be able to come back into his normal pattern with fewer obstacles – if he doesn't feel the whole world knows he left and is judging him for his "sins." If you are tempted to get revenge for his desertion by telling everyone, stop and ask yourself if you want him back. If you do want him to return, don't put up barriers he'll find impossible to hurdle.

YOUR RIGHTS

One of the first feelings you may experience when your husband leaves is overwhelming anger. You may start to rage about your rights! After all, he married you – and he "owes" you!

True, he has responsibilities to you and the children, but demanding your rights will not ensure that you receive them, nor will it help your relationship. That doesn't mean you should go forever without seeking financial support or finding an opportunity to discuss your other needs with him. Give him time to heal first. Right now he is suffering from an overload of obligations. Pressuring him about your rights will only make his struggle more acute – and you will probably get a less than satisfying response. Giving him time to heal is similar to allowing recuperation from a physical injury or illness – think of him as recovering from a broken leg.

Chuck had left home and was living alone in a small apartment – he needed "peace and quiet, and to get his head together." He continued to support the family financially and often telephoned, or visited them. Evelyn felt lost without him and was very angry that he left her with the heavy day-to-day responsibilities of four children. Every time he telephoned, she reminded him of his obligation as a father and husband. When he came to visit, she continually asked, "Are you ready to come home for good now?"

If he took her out to dinner, she would turn the evening into a big hassle of discussing "their relationship." Chuck began to contact her less frequently, sometimes not for weeks. Evelyn gradually began to follow our advice and stopped putting so much pressure on Chuck. We reminded her that many wives would be delighted to have their husbands keeping in touch as Chuck did. We encouraged her to keep each contact time casual, upbeat, and friendly. As she did so, Chuck began to warm up to her again.

But, you say, "He made a vow to me at the time of our marriage!"

That's true, but even good moral people do not stay married because of vows they made at their wedding. That may shock you. If you can't trust a moral person to keep his word, who can you trust?

But remember that a Midlife man is often in such an

emotional state that his own needs – which may have gone unmet for decades – are stronger than the vows he made so many years ago. He may find it easy to explain away the responsibility of his vows because he is questioning all his values.

INITIAL CHOICES

People generally don't stay married because they made vows, but because their needs are being met. Studies show that we choose to marry not because we wanted to meet the needs of our partner, but because we believed our partner would meet *our* needs.[4] Most of us, as young adults, were not aware of these studies when we chose to marry. As friction develops in marriages it is because our partner's needs have changed as years pass.

For example, your husband may have unconsciously chosen you because he needed a strong woman to stabilize his life. As he matured, he grew more independent, but you may have continued to make unnecessarily strong suggestions for his life – sometimes called "mothering." If you didn't withdraw the mothering, he has probably become irritated with your attempts to dominate.

We know other situations where men have married sweet little girls who leaned on their husbands for everything. The husbands liked this because it met their need to be a controlling leader. After several years of this dependency, the men grew tired of it and began to withdraw their attention. Then the sweet little girls became whiners, grasping for their husbands' care. But Midlife husbands generally wish their wives were more independent and growing as healthy adult women. In fact, the whining and dependency drives some men right out the door!

Their young adult need for someone to depend on them for everything has changed.

DETECTING NEEDS

Because you and your husband have changed in many ways since you were married – your ways of relating should change. Changes are usually subtle, so lots of communication is needed so you stay current with each other. People do not grow at the same rate, or in the same areas – so keep sharing your ideas, interests, dreams, doubts, and your very selves with each other. If you are alert to your husband's particular struggles as he reaches midlife, you can help satisfy many of his needs during this painful time of transition.

Some women ask, "What if my husband won't talk?" If your husband is still at home, but doesn't talk about his needs, he may be afraid you won't understand or care. Many men have trouble talking about *anything* that is personal. Think of the situation as putting a puzzle together. Everything your husband does and says is a result of his needs. Be a detective and piece your husband's needs together – you'll see the current picture of his needs.

Other women say, "My husband has moved out, how can I learn about his needs if I don't see him?" If your husband has moved out, you must piece together information about his needs from many sources. Spend time with a close friend who knows both you and your husband. The two of you may see some of your husband's needs that were always there, but that you had ignored.

What do your husband's changed life-style, clothes, habits,

and new friends tell you about his needs? If your husband is having an affair, the personality of the other woman should give you insight into some of his needs – and also possible ways you might change. Any changes you make, however, must really fit you, and not cause you to be uncomfortable with yourself. You can also learn what your husband's needs are by asking his friends to tell you. Remember, you are not spying on him – you are learning who your man is *now*, so that when he takes another look your way, you will be ready.

THE OFFENDER'S DEBT

Some wives have asked us, "Do you think my husband realizes his sinfulness and the terrible hurt he is causing me and the children?" Many women want to be sure their husband feels guilty for leaving. A natural human reaction is to strike back when we are hurt. Many wives want to be sure their husbands are paying for the pain the wife feels. A wife may not take any outward action against her husband, such as suing for divorce, or forbidding him to enter the house, but she may do everything within her power to make him feel guilty!

Sometimes women use children or health issues as a tool of punishment – "I can't get Amy to settle down at night, she keeps crying herself to sleep every night because she misses you." "Scott won't do a thing I tell him. And after all, it's a man's job to get him to mow the lawn, and check the oil in the car." "I have a terrible skin rash and I haven't been able to sleep or eat, so the doctor wants me to get a prescription to quiet my nerves. But I don't see how we can afford that now."

Producing guilt is not your job – it's God's. Your job is to make sure your own slate is clean – then do what is necessary to restore your marriage. Reminding your husband of his sinfulness and his obligations to the family will not do anything to rebuild your relationship. Don't even pray, "God, make him see how wrong he is!" Tell God all about your heartaches and then roll your worries and troubles over onto his shoulders. He promises that he watchfully and affectionately cares for you (1 Peter 5:7). For now, your focus should be to pray for God to change you where you need it – later, when your guy wants to return, you will talk about your needs, and he will listen then.

SUPER ANGEL

By now you may be saying, "Hey, that isn't fair! My husband is the one who left home and has been acting out in all sorts of ways. Yet as his wife I'm to be tolerant and accepting?? I'm supposed to keep checking myself for right attitudes and actions – and put myself out to be everything he needs?? You are asking me to do double duty!!! You are asking the impossible of me!!"

Sally and I have said the same things when we see the struggle some wives go through to rebuild their marriages. We have counseled hundreds of midlife men and women during the past 25 years, and we state – it isn't fair! However, we also have seen many men return to their wives, and have watched marriages be restored, when the wife was willing to walk the second – the twenty-second – and the two hundred twenty-second mile.

THE MOST IMPORTANT DECISION OF YOUR LIFE

You must decide if you want to stay in your marriage. If you do, then you have to commit yourself, daily and minute by minute, to put up with a lot that is unfair as you do your part to correct the problems. You need a strong, vital relationship with God, so that you will feel His presence during the tough times.

You will need the guidance of the Holy Spirit when you don't know which way to turn.

You will also need at least one good friend – or better a group – upon whom you can lean when the going gets too rough. Simply talking to someone else can help you gain a new perspective and help you hang on a little longer. You may need to be in touch with your friends often during the hardest times. Because the pain is so great, it's good to have several friends to share your load – so you don't wear out any one friend. Our chat rooms have been a great help to connect with friends to share the load. Many of these people are in frequent contact, and have become great friends. Again, the website address is www.midlife.com.

HOW LONG?
If you don't see quick results, you may wonder how long to hang on. Sadly, you may see your situation worsen and even take on new and awful dimensions. So the question is often asked, "When should I give up hope?" There does come a time when we will encourage you to be assertive about protecting your family and moving on – but we will talk about that later in the book.

There may also come a day when the situation is taken completely out of your hands. Your husband may sue for a divorce despite your efforts to prevent it. He might move out of state, marry someone else, and try to live a totally different life. But we have found that wives generally give up too soon – and it's clearly understandable. You are human and you get tired.

Exhaustion and frustration are two reasons why making

contact with friends is so crucial. You need friends who can be trusted to give you an accurate reading of the situation, and who won't push you to get a quick divorce. Your friends should not be easily biased to your side of the predicament, but should try to have an overview of the total picture, including your husband's side. Friends should be able to give you the courage and hope to hang on.

FRIENDLY BALANCE

Martha often felt she was at the end of her rope during her husband's midlife crisis, but her good friend Ruth helped her hang on. Ruth had gone through similar struggles with her husband a few years earlier, and she had learned that love and patience paid off.

When Martha got down, she could call Ruth and say, "I absolutely can't go through another night of wondering if Ed is going to come home. I think I just saw his car outside that big apartment building on Harris Street. What would he be doing there? I'm sure he's involved with another woman, and I can't stand that! This uncertainty is killing me. Maybe I'll just divorce him and end this frustration!"

Ruth had the right balance. She let Martha vent her feelings and then gave her bits of wise advice. And then Martha would begin to feel calmer and see more clearly. "I'm so glad I can call you," she'd say. "Thanks for letting me unload and for giving me hope again."

If you don't have such a friend, then read your Bible more than ever, looking for verses that tell of God's love and help for you. Books and CDs on personal growth and marriage can give you new strength and help you to grow and change. Growth and change in the long run – win or lose your marriage – will be a giant asset to you personally. You may also enjoy reading lighter books and articles just for fun to help restore your equilibrium. Look at our website for connections with trusted people, suggestions of books, and links to other helpful sites during this tough time.

Situations differ for every family, but your family will experience one of three general situations if your husband leaves home:
1. He may completely drop contact with the family.
2. He may maintain occasional communication with part of the family.
3. He may keep in touch regularly with phone calls, email, and visits.

Let's take a look at each of these possibilities.

THE DROPOUT

If your husband has dropped all communication with you or any of the family, your best course of action is not to chase after him. You may want to make sure he is well and safe, but after you know that, don't contact him at first. If you do, he may only run somewhere else. Or he may resent you even more.

In some cases, depending upon his personality and the reasons for his leaving, a husband may need to know that you care for him and that he is welcome to return home. But don't pester him. Choose the best way to let him know that you care. Do it, and then leave him alone. He will recover faster if you are not aggravating him.

THE DROP-IN

The family which receives occasional contacts by the husband who leaves may feel wounded every time. You need to pray that God will give you special grace whenever he contacts you so you can be fun and upbeat, yet wise, patient, and loving. Each time your husband gets in touch with you, you are being tested. How you handle the encounter will have a lot to do with his decision to return or not. Again, it may not seem fair. You are under unusual stress, and yet we are asking you to be at your best emotionally and spiritually. That is why you need to keep in vital fellowship with God and friends.

THE DRIZZLE

The man who keeps in frequent touch with phone calls, email, and visits seems to be having his cake and eating it too. He gets to have the benefits of home, yet the benefits of independence too. Some men, who have left, walk unannounced into the house, sit down for meals, watch TV, help themselves to snacks in the refrigerator, play with the children – and then leave again.

Shake off the feeling that you are being used and abused. Show him that you want to be his best friend and provide what he needs during this time of his confusion. Be sensitive about whether or not he feels like talking. Don't pressure him, especially about where your relationship is now, or when he is coming home, and so on. It is a good sign that he keeps coming to the house for short times. Women who never see their husbands would like to trade places with you.

SURVIVAL TACTICS

One of the best things for a wife to do, whether her husband has left temporarily or indefinitely, is to study his needs – and what made him leave. As you learn more about your husband and how he is changing, you will know better how to meet his needs when you have the opportunity. But be sure the needs you identify are *his real needs* – not simply what you think they are.

Suppose for a moment that I (Sally) want to show Jim that I understand his needs. Suppose he has been so busy lately that he doesn't have time to cut the lawn. I am embarrassed by its shaggy appearance, so I have several loads of decorative stone delivered and spread over the yard. Now, I think, he'll no longer have to mow the lawn, and I won't be embarrassed!

The problem is that Jim dearly loves green grass and growing things. He feels more relaxed in an outdoor setting with living plants. His real need is to have grass – mowed or unmowed. It's important that I understand his likes and dislikes, his values, and his feelings well enough to meet his true needs – not my embarrassment need.

Another example is Mary who notices that Joe would rather stay home and watch TV, or work on a hobby. In the past they would have spent time with their friends. But Mary has learned that right now Joe is bothered by the noise and busyness of groups. He needs time to unwind without feeling responsible to anyone. Wisely she is helping him get that time. His need right now is to be quiet and have time for reflection.

Your husband's midlife crisis is also a great time to evaluate where you need to improve your life. While you are going through this period, it is a great time for your personal growth and change! Let's look at a few of these areas.

Remember that men are "visual" — so work on your appearance! Look at your overall appearance — through your husband's eyes. What does he see? Is he attracted to you — or are you just expecting him to stay committed to your marriage in spite of the fact that you may have added 50 pounds, aren't keeping up with current styles, and you don't care about your hairstyle.

Also develop talents and abilities you may have been neglecting. If you have been a dependent person, learn now to be more independent. (You may have to become independent anyway.) If you have been a "nagger" think of alternate ways of handling situations that make you nag. If you have been careless about listening to your husband's needs, try to develop a keener sensitivity to everyone you know.

Take up a new hobby, enroll in an adult education course, or learn a new skill. Most husbands admire their wives for doing something to grow and develop, if they aren't neglecting other important responsibilities. What you choose to learn, or get involved in, may also be something in which your husband is interested.

But the most important thing for you to do is to practice *patience*. When it seems there is no change in your situation, be patient. When you wonder how much longer you can hold on, be patient. That doesn't mean you have to be a doormat and get trampled on, but it does mean that you will keep trying every way possible to restore your marriage. It means that you will work on the things you need to improve about yourself. It means that if you have the opportunity, you will work very carefully at communicating with your husband in loving ways and not pressure him in any way. *And you keep practicing patience.*

There are times to take positive action and we will talk about how to do that as we discuss assertiveness in a later chapter. Before you take that step, however, take every other step to help your husband, and yourself, survive his crisis.

WILL IT PAY OFF?

You may wonder if your patience and efforts of doing all the right things will ever bring your husband back. No one can say for sure. But everything you do to help him, increases the chances that your marriage will be restored. You and your husband have a history together that is going to be meaningful as he decides whether or not to stay in the marriage. His bond with your children is another magnet. In spite of all the friction common to family life, most people still have a desire to be in families. Your husband may want freedom from his heavy family responsibilities for a while, but eventually he will want to be part of a family.

If your husband is involved with another woman, another factor in your favor is that she probably will begin to make demands on him. She will push for him to get free from you and make a commitment to her. The carefree atmosphere of their affair will come to an end. The novelty of the new experience will wear off. If you have been growing and making positive changes, your husband may find you and the home life you symbolize increasingly desirable. Remember that his midlife crisis is temporary. Statistics favor the likelihood of your marriage being restored – if you are understanding and work at it. Hang in there!

Let all who fear the Lord repeat: 'His faithful love endures forever.' In my distress I prayed to the Lord, and the Lord answered me and rescued me. The Lord is for me, so I will not be afraid. What can mere mortals do to me? Yes, the Lord is for me; he will help me. I will look in triumph at those who hate me. It is better to trust the Lord than to put confidence in people. (Psalms 118:4-8)

In the meantime, while your husband is gone, or if there's turmoil with him at home, what should you do about your children?

9

LIFE WITH THE CHILDREN

While your husband is in the midst of his midlife crisis, you may not be sure if your children are a blessing or a curse! You might be tempted to say, "If we didn't have children, my husband would not have so many obligations and feel the pressure to keep going to a job he hates." You, too, would have more freedom. Perhaps you would have been a more attentive wife all these years if you hadn't had to spend so much time with the children.

On the other hand, you know you wouldn't give up your kids for anything! They are a joy to you and they provide some of the companionship you need during this lonely time. You must be sure, however, that your relationship with your children doesn't become a substitute for your relationship with your husband.

Life with your children, no matter what their age, gets complicated if your husband begins an affair, leaves you, or both. How much you tell them about the situation depends on their emotional maturity. You need to be honest, and yet spare them the details. Don't drag them through the whole gamut of your emotions.

TUNING IN

Your children also are hurting. They need time to adjust to the new situation. Even adult children living away from home suffer a loss when there is tension in their parents' relationship. Sally and I have interviewed university students whose parents had divorced within the past 5 years of our interviews. Student comments about family friction indicate how deeply children are affected by marital trouble between parents. Following are some of the student comments:

"I can't study. I just sit and wonder what went wrong with my parents."

"I hurt so bad that I can't stand to think about my dad."

"I feel so lost and separated from my parents, and my brother and sisters. It's as if I've also been divorced."

"I feel cheated. I don't know what a good wife should be."

One young man said, after learning of dad's affair, "I'm terrified of marriage and can't even think of intercourse."

"My dad says he loves me, but that's hard to accept – after what he did to mom."

"I feel like I don't have a home anymore. None of us kids matter to my folks."

I (Jim) have written a book entitled, *Adult Children of Legal or Emotional Divorce.*[1] My research showed that children suffer long-term trauma when their parents' marriage is troubled. Earlier studies suggested that children recovered quickly from the parent's divorce. However, studies which have followed the recovery process of "children of divorce" confirm the life-long impact. The deeper the wound, the longer it takes to heal, and this marital dysfunction is not a little scratch in a child's life, but a very deep life-time wound.

My book is about the aspects of the *emotional divorce*,

as well as about families where there is an *legal divorce*. The research showed that the emotional damage is the same in children whether the parents were legally divorced, separated, or living in the same home. If the parents don't get along – the kids will pay the price – often for all of their lives. Our website, www.midlife.com, has more information about this subject.

The solution is not divorce – it's working to heal the marriage so that kids have a stable environment to learn how to relate to people, and prepare for adulthood. Even if your husband has left the home without divorcing you, the disruption is still intense – and so is the uncertainty of what will happen next.

Young children often blame themselves when their father leaves. Reassure them that they did not cause him to leave. They fear that you might also leave. They feel helpless and frightened about being abandoned, so they need to know that you aren't going to leave them. They may not verbalize their fears, but tell them often that you will stick with them. Be alert to what is going on in the minds of your children. Whatever their age, look for times when they want to talk. This is a difficult time for everyone in the family, but open communication and caring for each other will ease the pain.

SUPER MOM

To give your children the emotional support they need – give them your time. You may be busy with your job, plus many new responsibilities, so you'll have to work hard at providing time. However, good quality time with your children is one of the most important items to include in your schedule. And don't forget that teens need your emotional support as much as younger children. Following are some things which we find will really make a difference.

Touching your children with lots of hugs and love pats is very reassuring during these stress times. Teens also need to be patted and hugged. Look for opportunities to put your arm around your child's shoulders and say, "I am really proud of what a great person you are growing up to be!" Touching will help your children to feel good about themselves – and assures them that you are not going to leave them.

Be sure you don't undermine your husband's reputation with the children as you explain what is happening. They need to respect him and love him – he will always be their dad. You can let them know the facts about what is happening between you and your husband without burdening them with details, or running down your spouse. If your husband returns home, life will be much easier for him, and the children, if they haven't come to hate him. Children tend to see everything as either all good, or all bad. Help them to understand their dad is not all bad.

You also are setting a pattern for them when they have troubles in their relationships. If they see you showing genuine love and kindness to your husband, they will be more apt to do the same when they face hard times with their friends, or with each other. Let them hear you pray for dad's safety and for God to lead his life. The entire atmosphere of the home will be healthier if you practice peacemaking and kindness in your speech and in your actions.

IDENTITY CRISIS

Childhood and the teen years are crucial times for the development of the self-esteem of your children. How you talk about your husband, or what they hear you say to him, will affect their image of themselves. Boys are generally protective of their mothers, but their self-esteem is linked to their fathers – so when the parents are in conflict, boys have trouble with allegiance. Girls sometimes feel sorry that their dad has to live alone in an apartment, yet girls also have problems with allegiances. If parents make derogatory statements about their mate, then the children's self-image is affected. Often teenagers in this situation will try to entirely escape the home and the parental pain.

Several studies show that the most well-adjusted children have a stable, loving relationship with both parents and receive regular visits from the absent parent – both parents help their children see that they need both parents in their lives.

For your children's well-rounded development, exposure to good parent models of each sex is needed. If your husband has left, you need to involve your children with male relatives or friends. Teens, especially, need to be around married couples who have strong marriages so they get a good perspective on their future roles.

Often children and teens get into serious trouble at school or with the law when the home is in upheaval. Understand the cause of the behavior and be as objective as possible in finding solutions. You cannot flippantly excuse the child's wrongdoing. Neither can you be unjustly harsh. Please don't blame your husband for all of the kid's problems. Provide security for your child even though your relationship with your husband may be very insecure. In several chapters of *Adult Children of Legal and Emotional Divorce*, we give specific coaching about how to meet your children's needs and to help your children cope during this time of upheaval – even if your marriage hasn't ended in divorce.

THE PROTECTION TRAP

Generally, there is lots of turmoil when a man is going through midlife crisis. Avoid the pitfall of overprotecting your children during this time when you might over-compensate for the upheaval. You may feel sorry about the emotional harm they are experiencing, so you could overreact by being overprotective. Some mothers move their children into the same bedroom with them. Others won't let their children go anywhere without them.

If this goes on for an extended time, you may keep them from experiences your children need in order to grow up and develop confidence. They need to be with friends, plus attend church and school activities.

The opposite of overprotection is to let them go completely unsupervised. Some women are so wrapped up in their own problems that they aren't aware of their children's activities. Not knowing where they are, or what they are doing, can be dangerous. They need to know you care enough about them to be concerned. As our daughters got into junior high and senior high, they told us of kids for whom they felt sorry. The parents gave their teens so much liberty that the teens felt unloved.

GUIDELINES GIVE PEACE

As difficult as it may be for you to get outside of your own troubled mind, you need to stay close to your children, their needs, and their involvement with friends. Maintain those firm behavior guidelines you have established. If your guidelines aren't firm, work at clarifying the boundaries so that your children have stable and trustworthy guidelines – then insist that they stay within those limits. Children out of control will only multiply your problems.

If your children have already experienced too much freedom and you realize you need to change the situation, do it carefully and gradually. If you suddenly start cracking the whip, your children are likely to feel that dad's departure has turned you into a tyrant. They are already in emotional upheaval, so sudden, tough discipline may cause them to rebel, become depressed, or suppress their pain – and it may cause serious problems later.

So if you need to do some modifying of family discipline, do it gently and gradually – but firmly and consistently. Don't forget to include the children in the planning of discipline guidelines. When kids help set the guidelines, they tend to be tough – and they will keep those boundaries better. Give them explanations when you need to enforce guidelines.

Another danger is spoiling your children by buying their love, or giving them privileges you wouldn't ordinarily allow. When you feel guilty because your marriage isn't running smoothly, you may want to make it up to them by indulging in treats, toys, clothes, and activities which are far more excessive than your usual family standards. You may also think you are gaining their allegiance so they'll be on your side, instead of your husband's. But the only person getting fooled is you. Even very young children know how to play their parents!

KEEP IN TOUCH WITH GOD

It is easy to fall into the trap of letting your family's spiritual life grow cold. You may question God's love for you in allowing this mess to happen. Also, you may be so confused and frustrated, that it feels as if you aren't getting through to God in prayer. Your state of mind may prevent you from understanding the Bible. If there has been a lot of yelling and bad feelings in the house, you may feel hypocritical to suggest prayer, or a family quiet time. You may even be too embarrassed to go to church – afraid that people may make cutting remarks about what has happened – so you stay away.

Remember that neglecting your relationship with the God is Satan's trap. Satan tries to make you feel worthless so you won't come close to the God. He makes you doubt God's goodness and power. The result is that you feel lonely and even guiltier. You forget to ask God for wisdom, and you go bulldozing around with your own ideas – in your own strength. Your children pick this up, and soon the whole family may be alienated from God. Remind yourself of God's love. Read passages such as Ephesians 1, Romans 5, and Psalms 23, 103, and 139, from a modern version such as *The New Living Translation*.[2]

Let your children see you reading your Bible and attending a small group. Pray and share Scripture with them, and talk about God's help and care for you. Don't let Satan deprive you of your best source of strength at this time. Guiding your children is a superhuman task, even under the best of circumstances. Let God be your ally working within them – and you.

PRACTICAL POLICIES

In an older book *Divorce and the Children*[3] by Vigenveno and Claire, we have found some very practical and helpful guidelines for working with children in a single-parent or two-parent home. These lists are rather extensive so we have moved them to the footnotes in Part Five.

It's too much to expect children to be able to sort out all of their confusing feelings on their own. It's also too much to expect children to create the stability which they need during this disruptive time in your marriage. The two parents need to agree on basic guidelines – so children will not just survive, but also grow during this difficult and challenging time in their lives.

Again, we strongly urge you to look at the practical policies which are laid out in the endnotes of this chapter.

LET CHILDREN HELP
Even though parents need to agree on common guidelines for the family during this time, children can be an extremely positive help during your husband's midlife crisis – whether or not he has moved out of the home. No matter what your children's age, they can help keep their father's stress to a minimum.

Let me (Sally) tell you about Jim during his Midlife Crisis. He went through a time when he could not stand the phone ringing, people coming to the door, or making decisions about our youngest daughter, a high school student. Becki and I went on a campaign to reduce tension as much as possible for him. We took all the phone calls and steered people to other sources of help – instead of Jim. If Becki's friends came over, we kept them in another part of the house. We tried not to hassle Jim with decisions about where she could go, when she should be in, and so on. As he began to heal, he was gradually able to be involved again, but we needed to protect him temporarily.

Children can keep the noise down, the music which dad

hates they can play in their own bedroom – and in general keep tension to a minimum. It is good for kids to practice being caring and unselfish. You can lead them to think of helpful things to do – a surprise car wash, the lawn mowed, or a special meal. Dad may not seem to notice, and he may even appear ungrateful, but teach the kids not to allow their emotions to go up or down based on their dad's emotions. Teach them to serve because it's the right thing to do. Tell them that someday he'll appreciate what they're doing. He will!

Our daughters were in their teens and early 20s when Jim was in the midst of his crisis. Barbara and Brenda were away at college, and Becki was still at home. All the girls were very sensitive to Jim's problems. In fact, they were sometimes able to be more alert to his needs than I was. They wrote Jim encouraging notes, showed affection, and did and said many things to let him know they respected and loved him.

Barbara, our oldest, cancelled plans for spending the summer out of state because she knew Jim was grieving because she and Brenda were both away at college. She had counted on the out-of-state experience for a long time, but she decided she needed to be around home to encourage her dad. As it turned out, she was also a big encouragement to me.

All three girls were a help to me during this time. They occasionally offered to take over the house, so I'd be free to spend time with Jim. They said things to raise my sagging self-esteem. They offered to do things such as go shopping or bike riding with me. They looked for ways to be special friends to me.

HOLDING ON TO DAD

Your children can be enlisted to pray specifically – that God will carry their father successfully through this tumultuous time in his life – that God will show him what to do about his work if that is a problem – that God will help dad find more leisure time – and that God will help with whatever their father's needs are.

Our daughters prayed often for God to help Jim. Often on Sunday mornings when Becki and I would be at home hurrying to get dressed for church, Jim would call from his church study to tell me he didn't think he could possibly make it into the sanctuary to preach that day. He felt like a hypocrite, preaching about God's power and concern for everyone – yet not feeling it in his own life. In fact, he wasn't sure he would be able to hold out against the compulsion to run away. Each time after he would call, Becki and I would stop everything to pray. We claimed the promise in Matthew 18:19 – "If two of you agree down here on earth concerning anything you ask for, my Father in heaven will do it for you."

We would plead with God to deliver Jim from his pressures, reassure him of God's love, and enable him to go on with life. Having Becki to pray with me had a lot to do with bolstering my own faith and ability to believe that God would eventually bring Jim through this wilderness. Those prayer times also helped Becki grow spiritually.

Your children can be a *great blessing to you* – as well as to your husband! Watch God work through your children to bless the whole family.

**Satisfy us in the morning with your unfailing love,
so we may sing for joy to the end of our lives. Give**

us gladness in proportion to our former misery! Replace the evil years with good. Let us see your miracles again: let our children see your glory at work. And may the Lord our God show us his approval and make our efforts successful. Yes, make our efforts successful! (Psalms 90:14-17)

Part 3
HELP FOR YOU

10

PEACE THAT EMPOWERS

Helping *you* survive and thrive through your husband's midlife crisis is the major reason this book has been written. We mentioned earlier that as soon as Jim's book *Men in Midlife Crisis* was put on store shelves, we began to get calls for help from women all over the United States and Canada. The very first call came from the bookstore owner, a woman whose husband was experiencing a midlife crisis. She sat in the store isle and read the book the moment it came into her store.

Email, letters and telephone calls, from wives all over the world, come with questions about how they can survive during their husbands' midlife crisis – and how they can help their husband survive. When we speak about midlife crisis at conferences, or on radio and television talk shows, most of the questions are about how a wife can help her husband – plus how she can survive.

Jim's book, *Men in Midlife Crisis,* was written to help both men and their wives understand the problem. Jim specifically wanted men to find help for themselves through the book. By acknowledging the problem, and learning that it is common to most midlife men, many men have been able to work on the necessary tasks of this transition time. That book gives men very practical help. Our other books will also help with the midlife years. *(See the **introductory pages** of this book for a list of the other books we have written.)*

So far in this book we have set the stage by discussing your husband's problem and how it affects you. We have also talked about your response if your husband should have an affair and/or leave the home, plus how you should respond to your children during this time. Now we want to discuss the strengths you must draw on, and how you can live successfully, while your husband goes through his midlife crisis.

PEACE WHILE UNDER FIRE
The foundation for inner strength at any time in your life is your relationship with God. You are strongest when you are experiencing inner peace. That peace comes only from being in touch with God. Circumstances around you may not be very peaceful, but you still can enjoy a solid, calm power within yourself. Of course, you cannot simply say, "OK, I'll forget the mess things are in and be peaceful!" Reality says that your life is in turmoil!! Following are some basic concepts so you can experience peace.

Inner peace comes from Christ – not from exerting your will and determining to be peaceful, nor from ignoring the situation around you. Jesus said, "I am leaving you with a gift – peace of mind and heart. And the peace I give is a gift the world cannot give. So don't be troubled or afraid" (John 14:27). Jesus also said, "I have told you all this so that you may have peace in me. Here on earth you will have many trials and sorrows. But take heart, because I have overcome the world" (John 16:33).

To qualify for peace, you must be "in Christ." To be "in Christ" means that you have accepted Him as your Savior. You recognize that He gave His life to redeem you, and you certainly needed to be redeemed! (Titus 2:14; Romans 3:23-24). When you acknowledge your sinfulness, and then appropriate God's forgiveness and cleansing through Christ's death, you are accepted into God's family (Ephesians 1:5-7). Being in God's family means that you share in God's inheritance – and part of that inheritance is God's peace (Romans 8:16-17; Galatians 4:7). *(Often in this chapter, and throughout this book, we will use the names Jesus, Christ, or God interchangeably.)*

Being "in Christ", means that you have been born again (John 3:3-7). You now have a new life in Christ as you now live (John 1:4, 8:12, 10:10, 14:6; 2 Corinthians 5:17). And you have eternal life for the future (John 3:36, 6:40 & 47; 1 John 5:12). In order to claim a relationship with God, you need the rebirth that comes from accepting Christ as your Savior. For some of you this is old news, but for others it will be new, or perhaps you've never needed God's help before. For each of you, however, this is *good news* – absorb this reality into your personal life. It is necessary for your eternal good – as well as for survival now.

FELLOWSHIP IS ESSENTIAL

Once you are a "born again Christian," you will want to keep in vital friendship with God so that His strength and peace can flow into you. You remain in a friendship relationship with Jesus much the same way as you keep in contact with a human friend. You talk to each other, spend time together, and if you do something to offend your friend, you ask for forgiveness. If you want to be close friends with God – do the same. The more time you spend with God, the better you will know Him.

What do we mean by, "Spending time with God"? To start, realize that God is with you all the time and you can hold a conversation with him at any time. You can practice a "God consciousness" so that in everything you do and say, you are aware that God is with you.

Create a special "God time" or "quiet time" by putting aside all other duties and thoughts. Your life is probably jam-packed with busyness, so schedule a regular meeting with God each day. That daily appointment will become a positive habit, and you will find it to be life-sustaining as well. Imagine that your physical life is only sustained by a regular hookup to a kidney machine. Now apply that same principle to your spiritual life. Your spiritual health depends upon a periodic and frequent hookup with God.

During these special times with God ask the Holy Spirit to teach you. God's Spirit can make the Bible understandable and meaningful to you. Read enough of the Bible each day to find some thought to apply to your life and the problems you are facing. If you have time for a thorough study, great! Use a concordance and several Bible translations and jot your findings in a notebook. If you don't have a long time to study, at least read some Scripture. Don't be a perfectionist – telling yourself you won't read unless you have time for a detailed study. It's better to read a little, than none at all.

New readers should not start at the beginning of the Old Testament, or try to read the Bible straight through. You will get bogged down! Begin reading the first four books in the New Testament, and then First John, Acts, Ephesians, Colossians, Philippians, and James, and then Psalms and Proverbs in the Old Testament. Use a modern translation of the Bible, such as *The New Living Translation*, so the language doesn't get in the way of your understanding.

AS NECESSARY AS BREATHING

Prayer should be a part of your quiet time with God. I (Sally), find it helpful, to first focus on God – his character, his great power, and his deep love for me. That focus leads me to a confession time, as I realize how unfit I am to come before him until I have admitted my sins and accepted his cleansing through Christ (1 John 1:9). However, I know that because of Christ I now have the privilege of coming to the Father with boldness (Hebrews 4:16).

Being aware of God's greatness, and His forgiveness, causes me to praise and thank Him for who He is, what He is doing in my life. Then I move to a time of petition for others' needs and for my mine. Whole books have been written about prayer, and if you need more help with how to pray, look at the article "How to Connect with God" found on our website www.midlife.com. You may also want to do a search on prayer on the website www.christianbook.com or www.lifeway.com.

During your husband's midlife crisis, ask God to show you definite ways to meet your husband's needs and for God's power to help you change. Then put feet to your prayers by working on the changes! You might need to control your tongue. Ask God each day, or several times a day, to help you not to speak when you shouldn't – and to speak appropriately when you should.

You might need to spend more time listening to your husband. Ask God to help you be attentive, and to arrange your work so you have time alone with your husband.

After you have talked to God about things that need to be strengthened or changed in your own life, pray for your husband's needs. But don't tell God to straighten him out. Instead, ask God to give him physical rest and mental refreshment. Ask for your husband to be kept strong against temptation. Ask God to make His presence very real to your husband, so that he experiences joy and relief from those pressures which have become so intolerable to him.

PRAY FOR "WHOM?"
Are you ready for this next suggestion? Pray for the "other woman," if there is one in your husband's life. That's a big order for you, but praying for her will be a step toward your own emotional wholeness. Ask God to bring her to a real living connection with Jesus, if she is not a Christian. If she is a Christian, pray for the Holy Spirit, who dwells within her, to guide her thoughts and decisions – especially regarding her relationship with your husband. Also ask God to meet her needs. Remember, there is a reason why she needs what your husband is giving her. I (Jim) have found that most affairs are the result of two very needy people connecting with each other.

And don't forget to pray for the Lord to guard your children against the instability that exists in your home right now. Pray for them to mature in every area – spiritual, emotional, educational, and social. Ask God to give them an understanding of what their father is experiencing.

God invites you to pour out your heart to Him. Psalm 62:8 says that we are to trust Him all the time, for he can help. If you had a best human friend who was wise enough to know what you needed right now – and strong enough to provide it, you probably would hold frequent conversations with that person. God is that wise and all-powerful friend. Be sure to talk to him often.

EXPECT TO GROW

When you keep in close contact with God over an extended period of time, you will notice that you are changing, both spiritually and emotionally. Look where you were six months ago and see areas in which you have improved. Sometimes progress is slow and you may not be able to recognize growth in yourself. Be assured, though, that you are growing and developing as you allow the Lord to work in you.

A sure sign of growth is "character change." Galatians 5:22 tells us, "But when the Holy Spirit controls our lives he will produce this kind of fruit in us: love, joy, peace, patience, kindness, goodness, faithfulness, gentleness and self-control." Each year you live as a Christian should result in you being more loving, more joyful, more peaceful, more patient, kinder, more filled with goodness toward others, more faithful, gentler, and more self-controlled. You will need a big fruit harvest of every one of those character qualities during your husband's midlife crisis!

Another sign of your growth will be that your commitment to God is growing stronger. As you see him faithfully working in your life, you will realize that you can trust him more. But often, during your husband's trauma, you may feel you have to look very hard to see God working. Sometimes you may be disappointed because God isn't working as fast as you want – or on the things you have outlined for Him to do. You can't tell God what to do, but you can pour out your concerns to Him. As you turn over more areas of your life to God, your confidence in Him will grow. Focus on your changes, not on how your husband should change – leave that to God!

GOD'S CHARACTER

Confidence in God comes about when you grow in your understanding of him. You might like to make a study of God's characteristics. Some of these websites might help you – www.biblegateway.com or www.biblestudytools.com. As you search the Bible you will see that God is perfect love, completely just, absolutely sinless, the ultimate in wisdom, and all-powerful. Add all the other superlative qualities you can think of. You will see that He is worthy of your worship and your confidence.

As you keep walking with Him in your daily life, you will feel that He loves you personally and is in control of this world. Yes, there is a battle going on between good and evil, God and Satan. But you know God is going to be the ultimate victor. The Bible says that "all that happens to us is working for our good if we love God and are fitting into his plans" – and "He who is in us is greater than he who is in the world" (Romans 8:28).

As you grow in your Christian life, you will see more clearly how Scripture relates to every area of life. Become familiar with the whole Bible so you can incorporate more of it into your life-style. Don't be discouraged if at this point you aren't well acquainted with the Bible. The time to get started knowing more is now. Study the Bible for more than content. Read it primarily to see how you can apply the principles *in your life today.*

ACCEPTING OR REMAKING?

Growth in your spiritual life is also shown by the way you relate to others. The more mature you become, the more sensitive you should be to the needs, joys, trials, and feelings of people around you. You will be more unselfish and more understanding of others as you grow in your personal understanding of God. Understanding that God accepts you just as you are, enables you to accept others as they are – without remaking them.

You probably know people who make you feel uncomfortable because they want to impose their ideas and beliefs on your life. I (Sally) think of a woman who always had conditions on her friendship with me. She tried to do my thinking for me. She would say things such as, "You don't really let your kids play in the rain, do you?" Or, "Well, if I were you, I'd tell my husband he shouldn't spend so much time at the church." If I disagreed with her, she got a sour, disgusted look on her face which was intended to punish me, or make me feel stupid. When one person relates judgmentally to another, the friendship is stifled. When you accept someone, it doesn't mean you condone or condemn their beliefs, values, or actions. You simply allow them to be themselves.

Your spiritual growth will enable you to work at loving others. Yes, I said "work." Real love is not an involuntary feeling that sweeps over you. Real love is commitment. John Powell says that genuine love is when two people "are willing to acknowledge and respect *'otherness'*[1] in each other." Each person values and tries to promote the inner vision and mysterious destiny of the other. Each counts it his privilege to assist in the growth and realization of the other's vision and destiny.

SPECIAL NICHE

Another sign of your growth is that you will become increasingly aware of your mission in life. When you know God more fully and relate to others unselfishly in love, you will sense God's purpose for you more clearly. As you evaluate the gifts and abilities God has given you, and the opportunities he presents for using your gifts, then you will know that God made no mistake when he created you to be the person you are. You are unique.

Recently, I (Jim) have been touched as I have been rereading the Psalms in the Bible. In Psalm 22 starting with verse nine, I was deeply touched by God as I read these words. "Yet you brought me safely from my mother's womb and led me to trust you when I was a nursing infant. I was thrust upon you at my birth. You have been my God from the moment I was born." These words were especially powerful for me because my parents' marriage was in trouble from the very beginning – and they really didn't want children. People suggested to my parents that if they would have a child, it might heal their marriage.

But I was not just the product of misplaced human passion – God was right there at the beginning of my life – while I was still in the womb. God was my God from the very moment that I was born – and he had a life plan for me, regardless of how I got started!

You are the only person in the world just like you. Think about it, no one else comes from the same position in the same family, from the same geographical area, with the same childhood experiences, with the same educational background, or with the same adult experiences. God has been putting into your life exactly the talents, events, and people He wants to make you what He wants you to be. Your job is to let "God be the potter." Allow God to form you, as a lump of clay on the potter's wheel, into the vase He has in mind.

Many people, through thoughtlessness or under the guise of humility, have never realized the abilities they possess. You may feel that if you aren't a great soloist, artist, or career woman, then you have nothing worth calling a talent. Being a good listener is as valuable as being a great stage person. Taking soup to someone who is sick is as important as preaching a mighty sermon! If you are not a leader, you can be one of the best, most cooperative helpers there is! The busy mother who can spend an extra fifteen minutes a day praying is probably more influential than the woman who directs the church Christmas program. God has special impacts for people's lives which only you can do.

SPECIAL NEEDS

There are certain spiritual qualities you will need – especially during your husband's midlife crisis. We have mentioned some of them throughout the book, but let's list them here, along with others:

- Complete trust in God
- Genuine love for others, especially your husband and children
- Kindness
- Serenity
- Patience
- Acceptance
- Wisdom and discernment

- Openness
- Honesty
- Selflessness
- Self-control
- Endurance

Sally and I are not looking for you to be perfect in each of these areas, but these are the goals you should be working toward. Sometimes I (Jim) find it helpful to say to myself, "Well, I think I am an 8 in endurance, but in trusting God I'm only a 2 – but at least I'm working in each of the areas – I am not a failure." I'm sure there are other qualities we could list, but if you are making headway in these traits, you have a good start on the spiritual stability you will need to hold up under the stress of your husband's midlife crisis.

The overriding characteristic you will need during this trying time is "endurance." Prepare yourself spiritually for your husband's crisis by having your own spiritual life in order, keeping in fellowship with the Lord, and continuing to grow. Allow God to bathe you with a sense of His love and care for you.

And then you will "endure until the end." Some days you will think you are at the end – the end of your wits – the end of your strength. But we mean the end of your husband's midlife crisis. You may literally need to picture yourself doing what the slogan says: "When you are at the end of your rope, tie a knot and hang on!" Make a fresh start each day. In fact, if you're like I (Sally) was, and you have a crazy husband like my Jim, you will need many fresh starts throughout the day! The following verse will help you.

And let's not get tired of doing what is right, for after a while we will reap a harvest of blessing if we don't get discouraged and give up. (Galatians 6:9)

You may also find these verses to be a help.

What a wonderful God we have. He is the Father of our Lord Jesus Christ, the source of every mercy, and the one who so wonderfully comforts and strengthens us in our hardships and trials. And why does He do this? So that when others are troubled, needing our sympathy and encouragement, we can pass on to them this same help and comfort God has given us. (2 Corinthians 1:3, 4)

11

STRENGTH, STABILITY, SANITY

Most women whose husbands are old enough to experience a midlife crisis have their emotional lives fairly well put together. Sometimes, however, that is not the case. A woman may never have sorted out who she is, discovered what her weaknesses and strengths are, or learned to control her emotions. Or she may have been fairly stable earlier in her life, but because of early menopausal chemical changes, unusual stress with teenagers, or stress which her husband's crisis produces, she may now be unraveling emotionally.

HORMONE HOLDOUT

Women who are normally stable can suffer very real emotional problems due to the estrogen deprivation associated with pre-menopausal or menopausal symptoms. It is sometimes hard to find a physician who will agree, because some male doctors, even highly trained gynecologists, for some reason ignore the estrogen factor and blame other causes. These attitudes only compound the depressed woman's problems. Sadly some doctors imply that it is "all in her head," or that she is not capably handling her personal problems.

Dr. James Dobson, a psychologist, marriage and family counselor, and speaker on the radio program, "Focus on the Family" reports that he repeatedly detects the same pattern of emotional symptoms in the early 40s women as women who are experiencing their climacteric or menopause in their late 40s. His findings have been verified by Dr. David Hernandez and Dr. Herbert Kupperman, professor of obstetrics and gynecology at New York University.[1]

Dr. Dobson strongly advocates the use of estrogen therapy, but warns that it is not a "miracle drug" for all the emotional problems of midlife women. His experience, however, shows that many women who are absolutely miserable and unable to function normally are greatly helped by the appropriate use of estrogen therapy.

Some physicians have been reluctant to recommend estrogen therapy to menopausal women. And some women have been frightened by negative estrogen information. Today women can expect to live twice as long as women 100 years ago. Hence, medical treatment for women must change to meet the challenges of increased female longevity.

Estrogen therapy is not a fountain of youth. Women with histories of cysts or tumors need careful monitoring. Hormone therapy does, however, slow aging and alleviate many degenerative changes such as the loss of calcium from the bones and loss of muscle tone and substance (which may even be misdiagnosed as arthritis). Loss of skin elasticity, which causes wrinkles, also can be postponed. Additionally, estrogen taken early in menopause may afford protection against heart attacks.[2] Estrogen can help with all of these changes in addition to stabilizing the emotions! Menopause is "treatable." Hormone therapy is a viable treatment from which many women can benefit.

Some of your emotional problems could be due to the chemical changes caused by menopause. If so, they can be treated. It's important to point out that your husband's erratic behavior can set off emotional reactions in you which have nothing to do with your estrogen level. (Please remember, your hormone level *does* vary each month. You are emotionally weakest at the time of menstruation because your estrogen level is also lowest then). We also need to acknowledge that other life-style factors, such as proper diet, exercise, and rest, can affect your emotions.

I'M OK

In addition to taking care of the physical causes of your emotional problems, you can take other steps to aid your emotional health. The first is to develop a good self-image. A positive self-image is formed as you understand and enjoy your uniqueness, and as you accept all God's work in you.

Many of us have been taught that thinking well of ourselves is a form of pride. We have mistakenly thought that "putting ourselves down" eliminates pride. The truth is that false humility can be a form of pride. We pride ourselves on our humility! But, true humility is when we understand our strengths and weaknesses – and then live within those parameters.

Gladys Hunt quotes Phillips Brooks on humility: "The true way to be humble is not to stoop until you are smaller than yourself, but to stand at your real height against some higher nature that will show you what the real smallness of your greatness is."[3] Of course, that "higher nature" – the true standard – is Christ. When we compare ourselves to him, we know the "real smallness of our greatness." However, it is also through Christ that we have the ability to be somebody worth something. When we give God the credit for "who we are" and "what we do," we are exercising true humility.

Thinking well of ourselves brings more glory to God, in whose image we are made, than does belittling ourselves. Loving yourself does not mean exaggerating who you are and what your abilities are. Self-love *does* mean that you have made a proper evaluation of your strengths and weaknesses and that you accept yourself as you are *at this time.* You acknowledge God as the source of your strengths, and by his grace and power you are working on any weaknesses that are correctable. Yes, you have a sinful nature and often fall short of God's standard for you, but you can accept his forgiveness and provision for abundant living through Jesus Christ.

Loving yourself means you value who you are, emotionally, spiritually, and physically. You may have what you consider to be physical defects. Some, such as your weight, can be changed. Others, such as the shape of your nose, are less easily changed. You need to accept the unchangeable and realize that God made you the way you are. If you have accepted Christ as your Savior, your body is the dwelling place of the Holy Spirit. Christ died for you and God the Holy Spirit lives within you – you are a valuable person!

YOU'RE OK

Jesus assumed we are to love ourselves when he gave this command. He said, "You must love others as much as yourself"

(Mark 12:31). Sally said, "A few years ago I suddenly realized that most of the time I wouldn't love others very much if I loved them in the same proportion as I loved myself. I have since found that as I love and accept myself, I am free to accept and love others. In fact, when I become aware that I have slipped back into picking on others, I find that I have started being critical and hard with myself. Then I must check what I'm kicking myself about, change if possible, forgive myself – or accept it, if it's unchangeable.

"When I am feel secure about 'who I am,' I can much more easily tolerate the faults and weaknesses of others. When I love and value myself, I love and value others. I am also more at ease around those who might be a threat to me, especially if I view them as prettier, smarter, or more capable. Appropriately loving yourself is a very freeing experience. You can enjoy so many more people because you are secure about your own worth. Your energies can be used for constructive activities rather than competing, criticizing, and backbiting. You also don't have to get worn out trying to remake people. When you accept them as they are, they will be more apt to accept you as you are. You also won't be under such pressure to impress others, or to defend the way you are."

THE GOOD WHOLE YOU

Hopefully, you and your husband have been building each other's self-image all through your marriage by compliments, appreciation, unconditional acceptance, and accurate feedback on strengths and weaknesses. Many of you, however, may not have been doing these building things, so you may have some deficits in your self-worth, now when your husband is less able to affirm you emotionally. For now, you may need to do your self-appraising and building alone, or with a close woman friend. Building your self-image will make you emotionally strong during your husband's crisis. This time will probably be one of the most demanding periods in your life. You will also be better able to help your husband if you have a secure self-esteem.

Our friend, Dr. Archibald Hart, suggests three basic steps for the development of a healthy self-image from which self-esteem emerges:

1. *Accept God's unconditional love*—"Our basic worth must be found outside of our human potential (or lack of it), and in God and His redemptive work on the Cross."

2. *Develop a realistic self-knowledge*—"Don't think you are better than you really are. Be honest in your evaluation of yourselves." (See Romans 12:3.) "You must develop a realistic awareness of 'whom' and 'what' you are, and this is where pride differs from high self-esteem. Pride is characterized by unrealistic self-knowledge." An insightful friend can help you get an accurate picture of yourself by lovingly providing honest feedback about your strengths and your weaknesses.

3. *Completely accept yourself: this must be done by yourself*—"Thinking one's way through to a 'sober estimate' involves more than just an intellectual look at your positive and negative qualities. Whether it is something you are dissatisfied with and can change – or something that is unchangeable – you must begin at the same point: *complete self-acceptance*. I am not advocating that you be resigned to your inadequacies. This is simply a step in which you

realistically recognize where you are now."[4]

You may realize you are impatient. Accept yourself as this type of person *at this time*. Accepting yourself as you are sets you free to begin working toward change, so that in the future you will not categorize yourself as an impatient person.

There's no bigger boost to your self-image than to realize that God accepts you for what you are right now. When you fail, God offers the forgiveness you need. He is also the enabler who helps you keep changing and growing. Christianity isn't a crutch for the weak, it is life and wholeness! When we appropriate what God has provided for us by a relationship with him, we find we have power, love, and self-control. (See 2 Timothy 1:7.)

MAD IS BAD

In addition to building a strong self-esteem, you need to control your anger during this crisis time. If you've already learned how to do this, so much the better! Many of us, however, have wrestled with anger most of our lives. As Sally and I said earlier, we have been taught that anger is sin. Anger is only an emotion, it is not sin. But what we *do with* anger can become sin.

If you've thought anger was sin, you may have tried to get rid of it by ignoring or suppressing it. Suppression will cause you to feel hostile to almost everyone much of the time — or you may feel unexplainably depressed. Suppressed anger can also erupt into physical problems such as ulcers and skin disorders.

Perhaps you have joined the school of thought that says you need to vent your anger and express it in whatever way you feel at the moment. You probably are finding that a lot of your relationships are disrupted as you do or say rash things you later regret. A lot of us, however, are in the middle. We don't regularly suppress our anger, but we don't usually give full vent to it either. We feel angry, usually blame someone else, maybe say a few angry words, or grump and stomp around until our anger wears off. Later when we think about the incident in calmer moments, we feel guilty and perhaps even depressed. We may do this so frequently that we are miserable most of the time.

The book, *Feeling Free,* contains detailed explanations about anger, and tells how to effectively control it. Following are steps you can take to deal with anger.

1. *Recognize your anger.* Pray for sensitivity and self-honesty. Make a contract with a friend, your spouse, or parent, to alert you every time you express anger.
2. *Release vindictiveness.* It is a law of our lower nature that we want to hurt back when we are hurt. *Forgiveness* is the key, and forgiveness of others is made possible through God's forgiveness of us.
3. *Express the anger.* Try following these basic ideas:
    - Deal with your hurts and anger as they arise, one at a time.
    - Accept responsibility for your anger – it is your feeling.
    - State your hurt feelings objectively.
    - Acknowledge the right of the other person to also have feelings.
    - Listen, receive, and accept any explanation or apology that may be offered, but do not try to force an apology out of the other person.
4. *Make a goal of trying to get understanding between the*

two of you, not necessarily agreement.[4]

DANGER AHEAD

To deal with the anger in your life, evaluate what kinds of situations most often upset you and lead you to getting angry. Try to avoid those situations or prepare yourself ahead of time if they can't be avoided.

When all three of our daughters were very young – age 6 to a few months old, I (Sally) found that I was getting angry with them at bath and bedtime nearly every evening. I would get impatient with their slowness. Later I would feel guilty for being "unloving" to them, and vow to do better the next night.

Jim helped me think through the causes for my anger and work toward solutions. By the end of a busy day I was exhausted physically and drained emotionally. The girls might still be very active and wound up, but they too, were getting tired. Our ability to be courteous and kind to each other was wearing thin. Once someone started being angry, it was easy for everyone to act negatively.

I also usually had work left over which I was trying to finish – diapers to fold, clean clothes to put away, dessert for a small group meeting in our living room that evening, and so on. I not only felt tired, but I was tense about getting the rest of my work finished.

Jim suggested that I get a short nap during the afternoon while our girls slept. Then I would be fresher for the evening activities. Jim also helped with the girls when he was home and sometimes took over completely. If he was not involved with putting the girls to bed, and was doing something that could be interrupted, he encouraged me to call him as soon as I felt myself getting stressed. Knowing I had a way out was a release. After I changed the pattern of events which caused my anger, I was able to avoid the angry feelings and the usual bad actions they produced.

HUMANS WILL BE HUMAN

Anger often comes from frustrated expectations. As we are less rigid in what we demand of others and ourselves, we will avoid some of the occasions for anger. Anger also comes from an unforgiving spirit. Much of my anger is because I expect people to be perfect. When they're not, I hold it against them. Imagine being angry because another person is human!

Many people have carried grudges for years. Instead of forgiving the people who have offended them and relinquishing their problems to God, they pile up grievances and become extremely negative. I wonder if learning to forgive isn't what makes the difference between a person who is difficult to be around, and one who is a delight.

Ephesians 4:26 is the classic comment on anger: "If you are angry, do not let anger lead you into sin; do not let sunset find you still nursing it." The Living Bible gives still more insight, "If you are angry, don't sin by nursing your grudge. Don't let the sun go down with you still angry – get over it quickly." The sentence concludes, "When you are angry you give a mighty foothold to the devil."

This Scripture assumes that people will get angry. But it cautions that anger is dangerous because it gives Satan a good chance to trip us up. We are much more apt to fall into sin when we are angry. One way anger becomes sin is when it is nursed and becomes a grudge.

Wives of men in a midlife crisis seem to get into more trouble with anger than any other emotion. Eleanor vowed again and again that she wasn't going to get angry when Dan sat around dejectedly staring out the window instead of getting work done around the house. But another Saturday would slip by without needed repair jobs and yard work getting done, and she could feel her anger starting to grind inside!

After several unsuccessful hints and nudges to get Dan moving, her anger finally exploded. "Why can't you do your share around here? All you do is sit and feel sorry for yourself!" But that wouldn't move him either. Finally one day he retorted, "If I can't have peace around my own house, I'll go somewhere else!"

He left in the car and didn't come back for several hours. That incident scared Eleanor enough to start handling her anger in a better way – she discovered that many of the jobs really could wait.

AMNESTY

During your husband's midlife era, you will probably have many reasons to be angry. Recognize your feelings, look for suitable ways to express your anger, and forgive your husband as quickly as possible. If he is irritable, withdrawn, or away from the house, you will not be able to talk it over with him.

Try this. Imagine that you are face to face with Jesus, and

that you are kindly telling Him about your hurt. Now imagine you are talking to your husband instead of Jesus – telling him the same things about your hurts.

Continue in a quiet meditative state and calmly explain your feelings imagining you are talking to your husband. Now, gently forgive your husband. If he doesn't know he has hurt or angered you, in your mind say to him, "I forgive you." When you are in a touchy situation and talking face to face is inappropriate, your internal attitude of forgiveness will give you peace in the middle of the storm. By explaining and forgiving in your mind, you are practicing so that when you do talk to him, you will be soft and ready to really communicate – not just be angry.

You can help avoid feelings of anger by reminding yourself several times a day, "My husband is going through a difficult time right now. I'm going to understand and help him. He has had to put up with me through some of my hard times, and he may need to help me through more in the future. I'm the strong one right now, so it's my turn to help him. Because I'm not perfect and God has forgiven me, I can forgive my husband for not being perfect."

Then pray specifically for the Lord to control your thoughts, feelings, tongue, plus your actions – and your reactions.

> **Have mercy on me, Lord, for I am in distress. My sight is blurred because of my tears. My body and soul are withering away. I am dying from grief; my years are shortened by sadness. Misery has drained my strength; I am wasting away from within. I am scorned by all my enemies and despised by my neighbors – even my friends are**

**afraid to come near me.
But I am trusting You, O Lord, saying 'You are my God!' My future is in your hands. (Psalms 31:9-11, 14)**

In the next chapter let's look at some dependency and independence issues.

12

Dependence, Independence, or Interdependence?

Questions always arise when Sally and I urge women toward understanding and affirming their husbands. Women react with anger or confusion, "Am I supposed to be a doormat?" "Am I to be his geisha servant girl?" "What about my rights?" "He promised to love and protect me all of our lives, why am I now being asked to take on this new strong role?"

ABANDONED OR SHACKLED

During your husband's midlife years you will be forced to think about the issues of independence or dependence. By midlife, some wives have become very independent of their husbands, emotionally and perhaps financially. Other wives start out dependent and stay that way. Either extreme can isolate you from your husband during his midlife crisis.

If you are too independent, he may feel you don't really need him. You may have developed such a separate life-style that you will have little in common. If, on the other hand, you are too dependent, he will probably resent you as a burden which he is tired of carrying, and he may withdraw from you.

If you have an independent nature and life-style, you don't have to give up your individuality and become a clinging vine. Work at being *interdependent,* so you can be a help to him – yet he can feel you need him. Discover what you each need from the other and what you each can contribute to the other. You know best what compromises will work with your particular personalities, careers, values, daily schedule, and the ages of children. You may not need to make external changes so much as changes in attitude.

INDEPENDENCE IN EXCESS

Naomi, who worked in the banking industry, has always been a very competent, optimistic, and strong woman. When Bob and Naomi got married, she gave up her career and took a lower paying job in a university town to help her husband through his graduate schooling. She is highly intelligent and a knowledgeable conversationalist on many subjects. Her husband, Bob, is intelligent, too, and has succeeded very well in his career. She is a vibrant, cheerful Christian who bubbles with sunshine and energy. She is one of those women who in her 30s effortlessly cared for her home, husband, children, and community events.

After her children were older she needed more challenge and began to work again in the banking industry. Naomi enjoyed the additional stimulation her career brought to her life. She was well respected and was soon given positions of higher authority at work. The additional finances gave her the freedom to buy things for herself and the family – that they could not have afforded on Bob's salary, though that was not the main reason for her working.

Naomi continued to care well for her family, but she naturally had less time for some things. One of those time-causalities was conversation with Bob. Often, it is the wife who most yearns for time to talk, but in this case Naomi didn't miss it. When Bob began to struggle with his midlife issues, he felt he was in the battle alone. His wife didn't take his problem seriously – nor did she seem to want to understand.

Because she found fulfillment in her career, she didn't notice that Bob was withdrawing. She didn't know how desperately he wanted her to need him in some areas of his life. He spent hours in introspection and his self-esteem was sagging. He felt his wife neither needed, nor noticed him, and his self-thoughts spiraled down into a deeper and deeper depression.

Now you think we are going to tell you he began to have an affair or ran off with another woman. No, he didn't. But he did go through far more lonely agony than he should have if his wife had been more tuned into him. Fortunately Naomi woke up to see her role in Bob's life.

Wives don't have to work outside the home to be insensitive to their husbands. They can be "Suzy Homemaker" all day and still be thoughtless and unaware of their husband's pain. Or they can be busy running the primary department in their church's Sunday school, coordinating an afterschool tutoring program, or planning the P.T.A. carnival.

Does this mean you shouldn't work outside your home

or take on a church, school, or community project? No, but prayerfully evaluate your priorities. Perhaps God wants you to temporally eliminate some activities. You might also decide you don't need to drop anything. All you may need to change is your independent, indifferent attitude toward your husband.

THE CLUTCH CRUTCH

At the other extreme is "Lena the Leaner" – (that's my [Jim] pet name for women who are insecure and too dependent). Lena's husband John was insecure as a young man and enjoyed keeping her dependent when they were first married. But now he is tired of the load and resents her clinging. When John tries to loosen her clutches, she gets scared and grabs tighter. That makes him resist her more. And the vicious cycle will continue until one of them breaks it – which will probably cause great pain.

You may say, "But God says I'm the weaker vessel and my husband is to care for me. In 1 Peter 3:7, the Bible says that husbands are to "Treat your wife with understanding as you live together. She may be weaker than you are, but she is your equal partner in God's gift of new life." This verse doesn't mean that wives are helpless.

Bible scholars do not agree on exactly what is meant by the word "weaker." Some feel that the word refers to a woman's social status at the time that book was written. The Christian message and Christ's example show that "there is no difference between men and women, "you are all one in Christ Jesus" (Galatians 3:28). Yet the Jewish, and surrounding cultures, had not given women the same social position and rights as men.

Other scholars believe this is a reference to women as being physically weaker. Women are weaker in physical strength than men, but women also live longer and have a greater resistance to disease than men. Other research shows that women are no less intelligent than men, and Galatians 3:28 points out that women are not spiritually inferior. In fact, the remainder of 1 Peter 3:7 says women are "equal partner in God's gift of new life."

Women also have responsibility in the world as God directed in the Garden of Eden, "Be fruitful and multiply. Fill the earth and govern it. Reign over the fish in the sea, the birds in the sky, and all the animals that scurry along the ground" (Genesis 1:28). You will notice that God blessed them and told them to "multiply, fill, reign." He called both the man *and the* woman "governors."

RESPONSIBLE INDIVIDUALITY

God's ideal woman as described in Proverbs 31 is not a weak, clinging vine. She is industrious about her household duties. She shops wisely and judiciously administers her household. This woman is an investor, making a wise purchase of land. She is an organized planner, and she is enterprising. "She is a woman of strength. When she speaks, her words are wise (Proverbs 31:25-26)." She doesn't sound like "Leaning Lena!"

If you are a Leaning Lena, remember that when the object you're leaning against moves, you fall over! You must learn to stand up without a prop. That doesn't mean that you turn your back on your husband and emotionally walk away from him. But there is a big difference between your being "one flesh" with your husband – and being embedded in him like a parasitic tick. "Submitting to each other" (Ephesians 5:21) doesn't imply mindlessness. If you didn't have a mind or will of your own, there would be nothing to submit.

MOMENT OF TRUTH

That brings us to the matter of assertiveness. When is it time for a wife to speak up? How should she go about it? Sometimes when Sally and I are counseling wives whose husbands are having a rugged midlife crisis, we often sound like a broken record. We so often say, "Be understanding! Be gentle! Keep patient! Meet his needs!" Wives ask us how long they are supposed to put up with their mate's craziness. If you feel you've taken all the emotional and verbal pressure you can stand, and you're on the verge of collapse or explosion, what then? Are there any safety valves?

Virginia was getting tense about the way Fred, her husband, was treating her. If he wasn't sullen and withdrawn while he was around home in the evenings, he was picking and criticizing. He would barely greet her when he came home from work, slump in front of the TV until he was called for dinner, and then crab about the food.

"You know I don't like tuna casserole. As much money as you spend on groceries, I'd think you could serve something better than tuna and noodles. Besides, the food bill wouldn't be so high if Steve (their son) didn't drink so much milk. And he doesn't need homogenized milk. He can drink skim milk like the rest of us."

He would rant on until he left the table to watch more TV. Virginia was so irritated with him that she would chip the dishes as she angrily cleared the table. The kids complained about how their dad picked on them, and Virginia would apologize and try to smooth things over. All the while her anger was building.

One night Fred complained again about the food they were eating. Then he started complaining again that Virginia was spending too much money.

"That's it!" she screamed and jumped up from the table, knocking over her chair. She stood over Fred, hands on her hips and yelled, "I've had it! You do nothing but crab and criticize! You sulk around here, expecting all kinds of attention and giving nothing but cold silence or dirty jabs in return! I want you to know that I'm not going to take it anymore!"

She grabbed her purse and car keys, slammed the door, and drove off. She sheepishly returned later that night. Fred's actions were totally wrong! But this was not the time for Virginia to press for her rights. Now don't become fearful if you have just exploded at your husband. Sometimes a good dose of reality relieves tension in the whole situation.

But generally, at the beginning of a man's midlife crisis everyone needs to give him a little space and tolerance. Later when Fred has resolved many of his midlife issues, that's the time to be strong and assertive, and insist that you seek couple counseling help to insure these problems do not continue.

Before you erupt like a destructive volcano because of your husband's erratic and hurtful behavior, learn to use safety releases to handle your tensions. God, friends, groups, and other women like you can be found in our chat rooms at www.midlife.com.

Furthermore, praise music, and relevant books also can be helpful. Later after both of you are stabilized, then it will be the time to confront your husband about one or several concerns.

WAR AND PEACE

There is a difference between *assertiveness* and *aggressiveness*. To be assertive means you express your desires or needs in a positive manner. To be aggressive is to speak or act with hostility. Assertiveness includes the idea of being bold, but gently confident about the validity of your message. Aggressiveness suggests a domineering selfishness with absolute disregard for the other's rights.

You'd much rather be *assertive* than *aggressive*, wouldn't you? To avoid resorting to aggression, plan ahead during calm moments and make use of safety valves, which we've mentioned.

After you've used the safety releases – talked to God, or a friend in our chat rooms, listened to music, gone for a walk, or read the Bible – then carefully plan how you're going to talk to your husband. Don't simply announce, "I've gotta talk to you right now!" Tell him calmly that you need to talk and set a specific time.

"A TIME FOR US" – TO TALK

Setting a definite time has the advantages of making sure that you actually get to talk and that you do it at a convenient time. Choose a time that is without pressure, not just before he leaves for work, or while the children are in and out of the room, or during his favorite TV program. Choose a time when you both are relatively rested, and when neither of you has not just come from another difficult situation, such as a tension-charged meeting.

Give your husband some idea of what you plan to discuss so he has the opportunity to prepare. Be careful to state the subjects simply and objectively so that you don't create an inflammatory situation as you are explaining what you want to talk about. Don't say, "I want to talk to you – you are being selfish and rude to me lately, and you're always lying about why you come home late from work!" It would be better to say, "Would it be possible to talk after dinner tonight? I am concerned about some of the changes I've seen in you lately."

If he should press you for more details right then, or become defensive over the mention of his changes, stay calm and quietly say, "Let's not talk about it now when there isn't much time, let's talk after dinner."

In the meantime, continue to do lots of silent talking with God. Ask God to guide your thoughts, to help your words be kind, and to keep your emotions calm, then you are likely to have a good outcome.

PRODUCTIVE DIALOGUE

When it is time for your talk, be sure to use a soft, calm voice. "A gentle answer deflects anger, but harsh words make tempers flare" (Proverbs 15:1). Clearly communicate what you feel you need to talk about. Keep the explanation short and uncluttered with details. No "rabbit trails" are allowed. Don't give him more than he can process. Speak slowly and choose a quiet voice. These actions will keep the conversation from becoming confrontive.

Be specific. Don't expect him to read your mind, and then be disappointed when he doesn't. Use feeling words such as "I'm puzzled," "worried," "scared," "upset," "concerned," or "disappointed." That way you're not blaming and accusing your husband. You are owning your *own feelings*. Your feelings come from what you are feeling – but you could be mistaken. Even if you are correct about how you see the situation, you are not attacking your husband when you say, "I feel . . . ," "I sometimes wonder . . .," etc.

Start your sentences with *I* instead of *you*. For example: instead of saying, "You are neglecting me," say, "I feel rejected and left out." Instead of declaring, "You always lie," try, "I am unsure of what the truth is." Instead of saying, "Your secretive behavior makes me feel insecure," say "I am apprehensive when you come home late."

When people protest that using *I* messages is simply manipulation, we explain that, although at first the method may seem mechanical, it is a way of helping us be courteous at a time when it would be easy to be discourteous. Using a soft, calm voice may seem like manipulation to someone who usually yells, but speaking gently promotes peace and doesn't make the listener feel he is being "badgered." Using "*I*" messages, as well as a soft voice, reduces aggression and selfishness, and is worth the practice!

"I HEAR YOU SAYING . . . ."

Check occasionally for feedback from your husband. True communication is not taking place if he is not listening, or if he's inaccurately receiving what you say. You might ask, "What do you feel about what I'm saying?" You may be unaware that you aren't being understood. If you assume your husband is thinking along with you, you may be shocked if he doesn't respond as you expect. You need to hear him say what he thinks you said. You may then need to restate and clarify your ideas until he understands what you mean.

In return, give him feedback on what he says. You might say, "This is what I think I hear you saying . . . ." Be sure you understand what he really means.

You may have asked for the meeting, but don't forget to also let your husband talk. He may react strongly to what you say, but hear him out. Sometimes in the middle of an angry outburst you may hear truth which he would be afraid to express without anger. He may try to sidetrack you with extraneous issues. Or he may counterattack by criticizing you. Acknowledge the issues he brings up, but gently guide the conversation back to only one main topic. Perhaps you can tackle the other issues later.

Following are some *don'ts*:
- *Don't* present your opinions as facts.
- *Don't* say "always" and "never" as they indicate you are exaggerating.
- *Don't* be haughty or sarcastic in your attempt to be assertive.
- *Don't* be dishonest; you want him to be honest.
- *Don't* forget to pray ahead of time for God's help in your conversation, in your decisions, and in carrying them out.

DOCILE DOORMAT

You may decide that being a doormat is easier than being

assertive and confronting him with your concerns. The problem is that most doormats wear out after a while, and the worn mat with the hole may trip someone. Even if the doormat is content to remain a doormat, she is denying the true person God created her to be. She is also failing her husband by not using the talents and opportunities God has given her.

Conflict between marriage partners is not unnatural. It's normal, neutral, and can sometimes even be fun. Nevertheless, conflict can become painful or destructive. Conflict is not good or bad, right nor wrong. How we view, approach, and work through conflict is what matters. And, to a large extent, our way of dealing with conflict will determine our whole life pattern.

If we speak the truth in love, then we are operating as Jesus would. It is the way of mature relationships – and it is the biblical way to care and confront each other in a respectful way. A doormat wife shows that she doesn't care enough to "speak the truth in love."

We are suggesting a balance in the above areas we have been discussing:
- Be assertive, without being aggressive.
- Be patient, without becoming a doormat.
- Be loving, without being overly gushing.
- Be truthful, without being harsh.
- Be honest with your feelings, without being accusatory.

IS MIDLIFE A JOKE?
Another emotional quality which will be an "asset" during your husband's midlife crisis is a sense of humor. You may say, "There's nothing to laugh at. I don't think it's funny at all!"

True, the crisis itself is difficult, but there are times when a sense of humor just might save your sanity. Appropriate humor occasionally can soften the situation for both of you. A well-timed pun might be one form of humor, or another would be the use of old family "inside" jokes. The old family joke may also remind your husband of the history he has with you and the children, at a time when he may be weighing whether to remain in the family. One of the most valuable forms of humor is the ability to laugh at yourself. When you are under strain, you can provide relief for yourself, and those around you, if you laugh at yourself.

Imagine how I (Sally) latched onto this statement from a *Family Weekly* article, when I read the title: *State University of New York Studies the Practical Uses of Wit and Humor.*

Their studies showed that "joking provides a very useful channel for communication on touchy subjects, which might not otherwise be touched without jeopardizing a relationship. A situation may be potentially explosive." (Sound like anything you've experienced lately?) The article goes on to say, "communication in such situations often can be safely carried out if connected to jokes, and kidding. Humor can enable us to touch otherwise hazardous areas."[1]

THE HUMOR BOND

During this time when you and your husband seem to have little in common, humor can build a bridge. If you laugh together at the same thing, you are forming an immediate bond together. It's a lot like cheering for your grandkids, as you both cheer, you are bonding – humor also is part of the way to rebuild a closer relationship with your husband.

Are you too old to laugh? Research shows that a sense of humor develops and grows throughout your lifetime. As we become more emotionally mature and able to see the funny side of life, we are also able to laugh at our own "strangeness." An evidence of emotional maturity is our ability to see something funny in our difficult situation.

AND FINALLY

Other suggestions for keeping your emotional stability during your husband's midlife crisis are:

- *Live one day at a time.* Measure time by moments, rather than days or hours.
- *Cultivate a positive, cheerful attitude.*
- *Don't be a martyr or a stoic.* Be genuine.
- *Be strong and weak.* Allow yourself to cry, but not in front of your husband. He won't have the emotional energy to help you. (Jim let me know that my crying would only increase his guilt, and he felt powerless to remedy the situation. He knew me well enough to know that in the past I would break down and cry when I felt hurt or unhappy.) I often watched Sally's eyes swimming, as she forced back tears. But during my midlife crisis I didn't have the strength to help. Now when I look back, I feel great sadness as I realize that I was unable to help Sally.
- *Remember the good times you've had together.* It's easy to think that things have always been bad, but remember your happy times.
- *Keep focused!* The Bible encourages us to, "Think of all the hostility [Jesus] endured from sinful people; then

you won't become weary and give up" (Hebrews 12:3).

You can be sure of this: the Lord has set apart the godly for himself. The Lord will answer when I called to him. Don't sin by letting anger gain control over you. Think about it overnight and remained silent. I will lie down in peace and sleep, for you alone, O Lord, will keep me safe. (Psalms 4:3-4, 8)

We've been talking about the internal parts of you – your attitudes about independence, dependence, and interdependence. In the next chapter let's look at some of the external parts of your life – your social and physical life.

13

THE FRIENDSHIP CONNECTION

In our research about midlife women, Sally and I asked how friends had been a help to them, or how they could have been a better help. The responses fell into the following categories:

Friends were *most helpful* who:
- Were understanding
- Didn't belittle the situation
- Had a big listening ear
- Kept the couple's problem confidential
- Offered unconditional acceptance
- Did not have negative personalities
- Promoted positive attitudes
- Kept in frequent contact
- Also had similar troubles
- Kept the children occasionally, so the couple could have time alone
- Included their entire family in their family activities

If the husband had left the home, it was helpful if friends complimented the wife on how well she was handling the children alone – plus they invited her and the children to activities. It was important for other men to spend time with her sons to provide model maleness for them.

WHERE ARE THE FRIENDS?

During trouble, friends can help you make it through until things level off again. Hopefully, those friendships had been established earlier – before the crisis. People usually rush to aid victims and show all sorts of kindness when there is death, sickness, injury, or calamity such as fire, flood, or tornado. However, if you and your mate are having a midlife crisis, there is usually not a rush of friendship. In fact, many people you might have counted on as friends seem to grow cold and distant when news of your crisis gets around.

This coldness is not because they don't want to be your friend, but they don't know what to say or how to act. I, Sally, speak from experience. Many times I have been tongue-tied when I've seen a friend at church, or in the store, or at a party who is in the process of a divorce, or another family trauma.

I, Sally, remember Beth walking slowly away from church – week after week. I knew she was in agony about her husband living with another woman. I often answered the phone when she called, crying – Jim was counseling her and trying to bring reconciliation. She knew I was aware of some of the problems, but I didn't know what to say when I saw her each Sunday – and I was the Pastor's wife. I wanted to let her know that I cared, but somehow I was so afraid I'd offend her, that I ended up saying little, or nothing.

If Beth had talked to me about her problem, then I'd have more grounds for a conversation. But many troubled people aren't brave enough to bring up their problems. And they shouldn't have to be the initiators. They are the ones who are hurting – I should be the one who helps.

I mention this so you will understand if your friends seem hesitant to talk to you. They probably want to, but they haven't had any practice talking to people with midlife problems.

Sometimes I don't say much to a troubled person because I don't know how much of their problem I'm supposed to know. If they have confided in someone else, their hurt could be increased if others knew more than they should. Perhaps your friends have this problem, too.

HELPING THEM HELP YOU

Our youngest daughter Becki is an amputee due to bone cancer in her left leg at age sixteen. As friends came to see her in the hospital after surgery, she realized that *she* needed to put them at ease. People would stand silently next to her bed and avoid looking at the empty space on the bed where her left leg should have been.

Becki joked, "Want to know how I lost 15 pounds in 3 hours?" Or "Wanna see my new basketball?" (The end of her limb was swollen and bandaged to the size of a basketball.)

She named her first prosthetic leg "Harold the Hairless Wonder" and told her friends, "Just think how much money I'll save on razor blades the rest of my life!" Now when she meets someone new, she usually brings up the subject of her missing leg, or her obviously artificial leg, so the new friend won't feel embarrassed – and will know it's OK to talk about it.

Unfortunately, midlife crisis with a family member may not be as easy to discuss. But try to let others know you are willing to talk about the problem.

Some friends may not want to bring up the subject of your husband's midlife crisis – because they are beginning to see signs in themselves, and are trying to avoid thinking about it. Others may already be in a midlife crisis and may feel it is shameful, or that they have failed spiritually. Remember, most of your friends are affected, to some degree, by midlife issues.

Friends will give you the extra support you need. But quality relationships take time. You usually can't develop them when you are in desperate need of a friend. Keep forming friendships with many people all through life. Your goal in making friends, of course, is not simply to have them on hand if you should get into trouble. Friends share common interests and are available to help one another. As you each unselfishly enrich the other's life, you will then be able to care for each other when a need arises.

Sally had two special friends, Roberta and Eileen, who knew a little of what was going on during my midlife crisis. Each of their husbands had also gone through recent upheavals – and Sally and I had been involved in helping them make it through their difficulties. These two women kept in frequent touch with Sally by telephone. She didn't have to give them details, but she could talk as much or as little as she wanted. They kept Sally encouraged and helped her keep a balanced perspective. Sally knew they were strongly supporting us in prayer – and that they weren't telling other people about our struggles.

INPUT AND OUTPUT

There are three types of relationships we all need, if we are going to be normal and spiritually healthy people.

1. *A person who cares for you.* You may not ever do anything in return to help that person. God is in this category. So might be your pastor, a counselor, or some other person who is spiritually more mature than you.

Our reservoir of emotional and spiritual strength will run dry if we don't have someone who cares for us. We need God to be filling us, as well as other human helpers.

2. *The second type of friendship is an equal relationship.* The give-and-take equal relationship is necessary for our growth and development as whole persons. You and the other person share, build, and care for each other in a give-and-take manner.

3. *The third type of friendship is when you help someone else.* Perhaps you will never receive anything in return. In some instances, your children are in this category, along with other needy people.

If we don't give to others, we grow stagnant. Additionally, we need to be pouring out what we have and know to those who are coming along behind us. I have noticed that when I begin to feel lonely and isolated, it is often because I am neglecting one or more of these relationships. I need some of each of these friendships to keep me balanced. If I emphasize only one or two types of relationships – I will be lopsided.

I (Sally) have mentioned that during Jim's midlife upheaval I drew heavily on God's friendship to care for me each day. I also had Roberta and Eileen with whom I had the give-and-take equal relationship. Events had happened earlier in their lives and I had been strength for them. But during Jim's worst year, these two friends had to bolster me – and I did little in return for them.

But I also realized that I needed to be helping someone else. Yes, I was doing a lot for Jim, but that was to be expected. I decided to start an informal process of helping young, single career women. Sometimes we went out to lunch together, other times one or two of them came to my home to talk. Often I would chat with them before or after church services. I helped them grow spiritually and emotionally as they wrestled with career change, dating – or lack of dating, roommate problems, and so on. Helping was a good outlet for me and added fulfillment to my life.

During this difficult midlife time, you will need all 3 kinds of friendship. It is not easy to care for others when you are feeling threatened and anxious. But if you can muster even the smallest amount of emotional strength to help someone else, you will find this act to be therapeutic.

There are always people to whom we can minister – elderly people who need a visit, a ride to the grocery store, or a light bulb changed. Some handicapped families could use help. Young mothers would be glad if someone occasionally took their kids for a couple hours so they could have a break. The church secretary or your local hospital can often use a volunteer. The list is endless – make a list that applies to your world.

You may be angry at God and reject His offer of friendship because you feel he has not been coming through for you. If he were a true friend, you think, he would change this situation quickly. When you begin to feel this way, read Scripture sections such as Ephesians and some of the Psalms. These sections will assure you of God's love and concern, even if your circumstances are not the way you would like them to be. You might find other Christian reading helpful. I would suggest *The Red Sea Rules*,[1] and *Where Is God When It Hurts?*[2]

PEER SUPPORT

Developing and maintaining good peer friendships is important. Hopefully if you have many of these before your husband's crisis hits. Naturally some friendships will be deeper than others. You need a few close friends with whom you can share your whole heart – and who will be available to hold you up when the situation gets desperate. You may have others who know your problem and will be praying for you and your husband, but who don't know all the details. You don't need to share deeply with everyone, and not everyone.

Remember to keep *only* women as your close, sharing friends so that you will be able to relate deeply without becoming sexually involved. The exception would be a pastor or a counselor – a trained professional. Your sorrows and confusion will be multiplied if you seek help from a male friend and the two of you become romantically involved. You are at a vulnerable time when your husband is not meeting many of your needs. Be wise and share your heart only with women or your counselor.

GROWING A FRIEND

To have a friend, you must be a friend. You can't expect to receive attention, kindness, and help if you never give any. If you have sown the ingredients for friendship, you will reap friendship. If you have been too occupied, selfish, or thoughtless to care for others, don't expect caring people to come out of the woodwork when you have a need. The good news is that it's never too late to start building friendships. If you have a shortage of friends, begin now to develop one or two in depth. Keep your motives straight – don't plan to strike up a relationship solely for the purpose of meeting your needs. A genuine peer friendship occurs when you each unselfishly care for the other.

Who do you choose for a friend? There are many factors, but this list is a good start:
1. You share common interests.
2. You are able to fulfill each other's needs.
3. Your temperament, intelligence, values, artistic and athletic abilities are similar.
4. Your commitment to confidentiality and openness are similar.

Many women find helpful, caring friends at our website Chat Rooms at www.midlife.com. These women have developed deep bonds and talk often by phone and email. But some of your best friends should be geographically near enough to you so you frequently can be together face to face. When things are really tough – right after receiving news your husband wants a divorce, or is seeing another woman – it will help if a friend can be with you.

FRIENDSHIP, NOT OWNERSHIP

Remember that your friend isn't your possession. Your friend may be your richest treasure on earth, but don't be jealous if she has other friends. As a mother, you know that when each child was added to your family, you didn't love the others any less – your heart simply expanded with more love. If your friend has other relationships besides you, she doesn't love you less.

There is another word of caution. Proverbs 25:17 warns, "Seldom set foot in your neighbor's house – too much of you, and he will hate you." You need to be with friends, but you have to use common sense about how much to be with them. Have an honest understanding so they can let you know the times when they must be doing other things. Then it's easier for you to let them know when you really must have their support.

Georgia had an unhappy marriage, so she found people to whom she could pour out her troubles. My Christian friends and I felt sorry for her and wanted to help – however we wearied of her long telephone conversations or personal visits. She was a needy person, but she didn't take her eyes off herself long enough to see that others also had needs.

She lived near Marjorie, and Georgia began going to her house every day. She would stay for hours, not caring that she was greatly inconveniencing Marj's entire family. They would come home in the evening from school and work, have dinner, and go on their individual ways again without any opportunity to be together as a family. Marj could see that the friendship was lopsided and unhealthy and that she wasn't helping Georgia to find any real solutions.

Finally late one afternoon Marj said frankly, "Georgia, I'm sorry, but you've got to go home now. I think that if you'd spend the time and energy doing things for your husband that you spend sitting in my kitchen, I think your marriage would be better. Your long visits are disrupting my family's life. You are welcome to come for a short visit, every once in a while, but I just can't see you all day – every day."

Of course, Georgia was offended and never returned. How much better it would have been if Georgia had been sensitive to what she was doing and not have "worn out her welcome." Georgia is an extreme example, but you get the point: Don't be an insensitive pest.

On the other hand, don't let this story keep you from contacting your friends when you need them. Your friends should have the freedom to let you know if they don't have time to help you at the moment. Having more than one friend will give you someone else to turn to, if the first friend is unavailable.

"A HELP IN TIME OF NEED"

A confidante, can share your life and will help you more easily transition major life adjustments. A confidante can support you, validate your beliefs, and act as a "sounding board" when you vent your frustrations, and keep your conversations private. It's essential to have at least one true friend during this crucial time. The proverb says, "A friend is always loyal, and a [sister] is born to help in time of need" (Proverbs 17:17).

FRIEND OR KIN?

Interestingly, many studies find that not many relatives are considered close friends. If a midlife woman named a relative as a good friend, it was usually a sister. Perhaps this lack of relatives as close friends is because in today's mobile society. Perhaps it is also because family members have not practiced accepting and affirming one another, and are afraid to let their relatives know when they are having trouble. Some women may not share their problems with relatives for fear of hurting them. Your husband might be their son or son-in-law, brother or brother-in-law, or nephew. What is causing you grief will grieve them, too. A friend from the outside is more neutral and less vulnerable to the pain.

When I was experiencing my midlife crisis, Sally did not tell our relatives many details. Our parents lived in other states, as well as brothers and sisters. After a time, in weekly letters Sally did begin to let them know that I was undergoing stress, but she was not very specific about my behavior. Sally asked them to pray for physical and emotional relief for me.

They knew when I came down with infectious mononucleosis and had a hard bout with flu later on, but Sally could not tell them about some of the strange ways I was thinking and acting. Sally didn't want to hurt them, or for them to think poorly of me. Sally also didn't want them to become alarmed and get involved in our lives with words and actions that would only have complicated things. Sally felt I didn't have the strength to cope with their emotions, too.

Had our relatives lived closer, they would have made their own observations, and they wouldn't have had sketchy information. As it was, they were supportive and concerned, even with only partial knowledge. They kept in touch by letter and prayed faithfully. The value of their relationship with us can only be measured when we imagine how it would have been not to have had their love and concern.

FRIENDS CAN COME IN GROUPS

Besides having individuals as friends, you will be fortunate if you also have a small group of people with whom you are close. The group might meet for Bible study, prayer, deep sharing, a work project, or a community task. The important thing is that you regularly touch each other's lives in some meaningful way. They may be people with whom you can share your hurts and anxieties about your husband.

It is riskier to share your problems in a group, though, because you need to know how much you can trust each one. Some will be more affirming than others. You may decide that it isn't appropriate to share with the entire group, but meeting with them will still be meaningful to you.

Activities with a group provide the stimulation, input, and outlet that you need to keep you from becoming too absorbed with your problems. From the group you may find some of the few close friends when the group isn't meeting.

Earlier we mentioned Donna who stayed in the denial stage too long, after her husband asked for a divorce, she tried to commit suicide. Then Donna got into a small Bible sharing group where she received lots of support. She could pour out her feelings and fears at the meetings, and to individuals during the week. Some group members took her and her children for family picnics, miniature golfing, and church socials. Their care helped her through the rough time of adjustment during and after her divorce.

VULNERABLE LOVE

The key to successful friendships is in finding people with whom you can be open, honest, and affirming. But you must be willing to be vulnerable. For you to continue your openness and honesty, they also need to be open and honest. Ideally, as you affirm them, they will support and help you. There will be times when you receive more from them than you give to them, but other times the process is reversed. Your model for sacrificial love and acceptance is Jesus Christ. As you study the first four books of the New Testament, you will be awed by Jesus' unconditional love.

Christ's unconditional love was wonderfully expressed with that "impulsive, uneducated, smelly fisherman" Peter – that aspiring "water walker" who started to sink – that "tempter" who wanted to thwart Christ's Jerusalem mission – that "ear-slashing" hero who had fallen asleep while watching and praying with Christ – that "dogmatic" friend who vehemently swore that he didn't even know Christ – that "ministry dropout" who went back to his old ways when Christ seemed to have left the scene. Christ poured his love on Peter. Jesus entrusted Peter with responsibility, chased him out several times, and always dealt with him in love. He saw potential in Peter and enabled him to develop into a dynamic, useful servant.

Bruce Larson has been one of many powerful voices teaching us that we must become "radically vulnerable and radically affirmative" toward other people. Yes, this will be costly, and we may often fail. But the more we guard our lives and protect ourselves, the more lonely – and withdrawn, we will become.[3]

As you develop relationships, you will experience personal growth and have a friend's help in troubled times – as well as know the joy of enriching someone else's life. As you reach out to add worth and meaning to someone else's life, your own worth and meaning will be increased. Accepting your friend's love, and as you in turn love your friend unconditionally, you also begin to experience a tiny bit of how much Christ loves and accepts you. When a "friend with skin" sacrifices time and emotional energy to meet your needs, that person helps you to understand a little more about Christ's sacrifice for you.

Quality friendships are invaluable at any time, but especially during the stress and pressures of your husband's midlife crisis. Quality friendships will also teach you how to be a true friend to your husband at this crucial time.

> **"Love prospers when a fault is forgiven, but dwelling on it separates close friends." (Proverbs 17:9)**
> **"A friend is always loyal, and a brother is born to help in time of need." (Proverbs 17:17)**
> **"There are 'friends' who destroy each other, but a real friend sticks closer than a brother." (Proverbs 18:24)**
> **"A truly wise person uses few words; a person with understanding is even-tempered." (Proverbs 17:27)**

Other important factors influencing how well you manage during this time are your physical health and appearance, so what can you do about them? Let's look at these in the next chapter.

14

OLDER, BUT BETTER!

Sally wrote this fun bit of verse which carries a lot of painful truth.

"You're not getting older – you're just getting better,"
They whispered with a grin.
But if I am getting better,
Why do I have to suck my stomach in?

If I'm getting better, and not getting older,
Why do they offer me,
Dye for my hair, creams for my skin,
And B12 to boost my energy?

If I'm getting better, and not getting older,
Why do I feel morose
When my feet and ankles swell
And I see all my veins are varicose?

If I'm getting better, and not getting older,
Why do they laugh and jeer

> When I begin to pant and fan
> And ask why it is so hot in here?
>
> Since I'm getting better and not getting older,
> My higher self decides
> To develop inner beauty.
> But, Lord, couldn't I look sexy besides?[1]

Like it or not, midlife women are caught in a race with age and beauty. It's a difficult balance between spending hours and fortunes trying to maintain or regain beauty – or giving up completely. Women tell themselves, "It's who we are that counts." But most women know that men are very visual and they do notice how women look – and that includes our husbands. Women feel much better if they feel physically attractive. The outside appearance does influence the inside qualities, and vice versa.

THE ENEMY

Women may spend hundreds of dollars on cosmetics, hair, clothes, and even cosmetic surgery – but there is still that relentless enemy – age! Some of us are more successful in hiding it than others, but as time marches on, so do the wrinkles and fat rolls! You may diet and exercise until you are red in the face, but your aging progresses relentlessly. Some women, in frustration, quit dieting and exercising, but aging never quits.

Women at midlife, more than at any other time, are obsessively concerned with their appearance because they equate attractiveness with youthfulness. Since midlife women think they are no longer youthful, they may conclude they are no longer attractive. And our world places a strong emphasis on being attractive. We constantly hear, "You must be attractive to win your husband and keep him. You must be attractive if you are working outside your home. You must be attractive if you wish to be respected at the church, community, or school." The pressure is always there – even in Christian circles. Looking good and being in shape isn't all bad, but you can certainly lose your perspective about what is, and isn't important.

A lot of the dilemma comes from the societal stereotype of midlife women. Women with wrinkles and sagging shapes are considered ugly and even repulsive, while midlife men with gray hair – or no hair at all – and a thickening waistline are often considered "mature" and desirable. This exaggerates the problem for the midlife wife whose husband may be looking at younger women – who may find him attractive. Eventually a wife will come through this time, as she accepts her appearance – and her husband will feel more content to be who he is – aged, wrinkled, and out of shape. But during midlife, many women live in agony over their physical appearance.

PASSING YOUTH — SAGGING WORTH

According to research, midlife women judge their worth by their appearance more than women of any other age group. They also seem less able to value their qualities objectively, especially if they only focus on the loss of youthfulness. If a woman's value is in her beauty, and beauty is most often identified with young adults, then the aging process steals away a woman's value and her self-esteem.

This researcher also points out that men are permitted 2 contradicting standards of physical attractiveness – his social power, and his aging physical body. A man's desirability is enhanced by signs of aging – plus his power, wealth, and achievement often increase with age. Women are permitted only one standard – attractiveness associated with youthfulness. So, you can see why it is easy for an aging woman to resent this age. But, have you noticed something? Nobody, who lives past their 20s, keeps the body of a twenty-something. What are we to do? Give up? Fight harder? What should be the Christian woman's attitude?

INNER LOVELINESS – OUTER UGLINESS

In spite of our culture's glorification of youth and beauty, many people realize there is more to a woman than her exterior. Men may be attracted initially to a pretty, young woman, but if her spirit is ugly and selfish, they lose interest. But some women excuse their overweight bodies, stringy hair, and non-descript faces by playing the "beautiful soul" card. Why can't beautiful souls come in attractive containers? Really, there is no excuse for packaging the Spirit of God in an out of shape, bulky wrapper. You are not necessarily a vain person if you watch your weight, care for your hair and face, and dress attractively.

You may have some "givens" which you don't consider ideal and which can't be easily changed, such as a short chin or closely set eyes. But most of us could do a lot more with what we have than we do. I'm sure right now you can think of women who have unattractive facial features but who have learned to create beauty with makeup and hairstyle. On the other hand, you know ordinary women who could be beautiful if they used makeup appropriately, and styled their hair. Making the most of your physical appearance is good stewardship, the same as making good use of time or talents.

I think of Holly who looked boring and drab. Her hair was clean but blah. She wore no makeup because she felt Christian women shouldn't. There was nothing wrong with her clothes – if she'd been wearing them a decade earlier. When she started working part-time in an office with other women, she realized that her husband lived all day around attractive women who generally were on their best behavior.

She gradually began to change her appearance so that today she is a very appealing woman. Her hair is in a bouncy, attractive style. She wears a moderate amount of makeup which enhances her warm eyes and smile. Her clothes are appropriate and accented with contemporary accessories. The new Holly is also more outgoing and friendly because she feels confident about her appearance.

HUMAN ECOLOGY

God is the creator of beauty. We are all for preserving and appreciating the beauty of nature – woods, grasslands, flowers, sky, rivers and lakes, birds and animals. The human body is also part of God's creation, and it isn't wrong to preserve, groom, and appreciate that part of God's handiwork, too.

Our body is also the temple of the Holy Spirit, if we are God's children. The temple that Solomon built for God, as described in 1 Kings 5:2-6:38, was no dumpy hovel built from leftover scraps! The finest materials were used by the most skilled craftsmen. Even the tabernacle, the temporary dwelling place of God while the Israelites wandered in the desert for forty years, was carefully and beautifully made from costly materials (Exodus 35:4-39, 42). Doesn't it seem appropriate to do this as well with our human body? The Bible says that our bodies are the temples of God.

Of course, any good thing can be overdone – or underdone – and then become sin. You can spend too much time, thought, and money on your physical appearance. We are warned not to be "concerned about the outward beauty that depends on jewelry, or beautiful clothes, or hair arrangement" (1 Peter 3:3). The meaning here is not to be *overly concerned* and not to depend on the outward trappings to make real beauty. The Amplified New Testament and New American Standard Bible use the phrase, "*merely external.*"

The Bible is not suggesting that women not wear jewelry or clothing, or the Bible might be seen as be advocating nudity! This is merely a warning against the wearing of *fine* jewelry and *fine* clothes – "outward adornment" that detract from true beauty.

The emphasis is to be on the inner qualities named in the verse that follows, "Instead, it should be that of your inner self, the unfading beauty of a gentle and quiet spirit, which is of great worth in God's sight" (1 Peter 3:4). You can possess the lasting beauty of a gentle and quiet spirit by knowing and reflecting Jesus. If you have a plain face and your figure could be better, you can still be beautiful when your face and attitudes mirror the sweet disposition of Jesus.

FIGHTING THE BATTLE
There are some specific things you can do to maintain, or regain, your physical attractiveness. Almost every newspaper and magazine for women contains hints on diet, exercise, and care for skin and hair. We get so used to seeing these articles and the advertisements that we almost become immune, or so

confused that we don't know what to do first. Many women just do nothing.

Let your common sense help you. Perhaps you can recall the health books you studied in school stressed proper diet, rest, fresh air, exercise, and cleanliness as being important to health and a healthy appearance. Those concepts would be good places to start.

There are many books which provide definite direction in each of the areas such as, fashion, makeup techniques, hair care, diet, exercise, poise, menopause, as well as face-lifts and challenges for your sex life. When Sally saw sections on makeup and fashion in one book, I thought I wouldn't bother to buy the book because trends in those areas change quickly. As I read further, I saw that her advice will still be valid long after fads and trends have changed many times.

If you need help in this area, you might look at a book which a friend of ours has written entitled, *Color Me Beautiful*. Carole Jackson's book was the *New York Times* best seller for four years, and it is still in bookstores, because it is not built on fads – but on the woman's unique face and body.[2]

WORDS TO THE WISE

You need to strike a balance between making yourself physically attractive and emotionally and spiritually vibrant. Keep your mind and heart in the Scriptures but remember you want your earthly temple to reflect the Lord. On the other hand, don't use spirituality as an excuse for being dumpy and drab. I (Sally) really appreciate Christian writers such as Angela Thomas[3] and Stasi Eldrige[4] who advocate physical attractiveness and show how to develop true inner, spiritual beauty.

We'll assume you are already working on the spiritual and emotional parts of yourself. Let's now take a quick look at some areas of your physical appearance you can improve. Perhaps you will get stimulated to do more serious study and work on your weak areas. That will make you more attractive to your husband – and yourself! Remember, your husband is a visual "critter" – and there are lots of women who are willing to look good for him.

First of all, you need a healthy, rested body. By this time in life, you probably know how many hours of sleep you need each night to feel rested. The number of hours in bed isn't as important, as whether you are truly rested during those hours. If you are having trouble sleeping, try deliberately giving all your cares to the Lord as you go off to sleep. Let God run the world for a few hours.

If there are physical reasons why you can't sleep, get help from your physician. A word of caution, however – some medical doctors quickly prescribe sleeping pills which can cause dependency, or other ill effects. Ask your doctor to help you with other remedies before you resort to sleeping pills. Vigorous exercise during the day or early evening, and drinking milk or a warm non-stimulating drink at bedtime may help. You need an adequate amount of sleep to be at your best. Problems seem monumental when you are tired, but they are much smaller when you are rested.

See a doctor once a year for your Pap smear and annual physical. Since cervical cancer is one of the most common forms of cancer among women, and yet one of the easiest to treat if detected early, it is disrespectful toward God's temple not to get an annual Pap smear. You are the one to make and keep the appointment. Your children may nag you to get some cuter clothes or change your hairstyle, but not too many people will check to see if you have had your annual physical exam.

Additionally, give yourself a regular breast examination while you're taking your morning shower. If you don't know how, ask your doctor to give you a pamphlet to teach you. Or find the information on the internet, or at your library.

BODY CHEMISTRY

At midlife your physical health and emotional well-being are affected by your diet. What you eat affects not only your weight and figure, but also your energy, emotional resilience, and other aspects of your health. Your need for healthy eating and even supplemental vitamins is greatly increased because of the tremendous stress on your body during this time.

If you ask some doctors about vitamins, they may smile condescendingly and say, "Now, Mrs. Midlife, you get all the vitamins you need from a balanced diet." Or, as one doctor told Sally, "You can spend your money on vitamins if you want to, but it's like pouring water on sand!"

Medical doctors have a history of denying the nutritional approach to physical and emotional health. It seems that until recently the medical profession has not taken time for much research in this area – and they would not accept the results achieved by others.

Fortunately, more medical doctors are now receiving training in nutrition and recognize its tremendous contribution to health. If your doctor isn't one of them, we recommend you find a new doctor.

One of the problems of our so-called "balanced diet" is that much of the nutritional value is lost in the processing and cooking, either in our kitchens or before it reaches our homes. Our food isn't doing us the good it should, plus our bodies are in greater need at midlife. There are lots of sources on the internet to give you coaching on proper food, vitamin supplements and the value of "raw" foods.

It's also good to see the first lady, Michelle Obama, take a strong stand for better nutrition for our children. Food companies and schools are feeling the pressure to do something about childhood obesity – this is a great healthy direction for our country.

Some time ago I (Sally) was having trouble with water retention. Two doctors gave me diuretics. I felt extremely weak whenever I took those prescriptions, so I ate more food to try and compensate for the energy loss. I still didn't have much pep, so I didn't exercise much. The extra food very quickly accumulated as fat. So now I was heavier from fat and extra water! And I still lacked energy.

Finally, a diffcrent doctor took a genuine interest in my situation. Instead of handing me another drug prescription, he did a careful analysis of my blood chemistry and the various prescriptions and self-prescribed vitamins I was taking. On that basis he decided what deficiencies I had and what vitamins and minerals I needed to supplement my diet. It was not long before I felt healthier and more energetic than I had in years – plus I lost some of the weight.

DIVIDENDS FROM EXERCISE

Exercise is also important for your health. You may think that the exercise you get while up with your kids or with your career is sufficient. Unless you have nearly quit eating, it isn't. Even if your weight is what you want it to be, then you need to exercise for more than just burning off calories. You need to condition your body, tone your muscles, and increase your oxygen processing.

Why do we mention oxygen processing? Oxygen is the key in converting the food you eat into energy. Your energy level is dictated by your body's ability to get and process oxygen. If you have a well-developed oxygen processing system, you burn your fuel (food) quickly and efficiently to produce energy. This system is made up of efficient lungs, a powerful heart, and a good vascular system. You contribute to their effectiveness by regularly exercising in a way that forces your body to breathe hard – and process oxygen rapidly – for 10 to 15 minutes – at least three times a week. Exercise that makes you breathe hard over a period of time is called "aerobic" exercise.

You should start into any exercise program gradually, and make sure your doctor approves of any strenuous conditioning program. There are many workable suggestions on the internet for particular trouble spots for midlife women – bust line, waistline, midriff, upper arms, and so on.

Exercise will also benefit your emotional well-being during

your husband's midlife crisis. Frustrations seem to lessen after a long, brisk walk or other vigorous exercise. Aggressive feelings find a safe outlet through physical exertion. Many counselors have found that the midlife woman's emotional state greatly improves with regular, strenuous exercise. Being faithful about exercise and diet contribute to self-approval and that good feeling you get from being self-disciplined. Plus your improved physical appearance will also give you more confidence.

YOUR MAN IS LOOKING

You might say, "Well, I'm in favor of all those health hints you've mentioned because I believe in doing my part to have a healthy body. But I'm not so sure that my body appearance, fashion, makeup techniques, and hairstyle are important as long as I am focusing on being a godly woman."

But remember, you are a steward of all that God has entrusted to you, and that includes your physical appearance.

An important consideration, especially at midlife, is how your appearance affects your husband. Since he is going through a giant upheaval as he rethinks his values and commitments, he is probably looking through a different lens. How does he think you look? Do you dress to suit him? Are you sexually appealing? What does he like or dislike about your figure?

Perhaps he hasn't told you what he thinks for a long time. But you may have a good idea of what he likes and dislikes in a woman's appearance. Study his tastes. From your observations and his past subtle comments, you can probably piece together a pretty complete picture of what appeals to him – what turns him on? Then do what you can to improve what you have. God wants you to meet your husband's needs in the area of physical attractiveness.

IS DOWDINESS NEXT TO GODLINESS?

You already know that how you dress is one of the keys to your physical appearance. Even if your clothing budget is small, you can capitalize on what is complimentary to you. It is better to have a few things that look good on you, than closets full of inappropriate clothes.

Some Christian women feel that, most of all they should not follow the current fashions. Somehow wearing clothes that are five to ten years behind style is godlier. The interesting point is that 5 or 10 years ago some people considered *those* clothes "worldly!"

There are some good reasons for wearing current fashions, one of which is to make you look and feel younger. Some people act as if it were more spiritual to look old. In fact, during this time when your husband may be struggling with being attracted to younger women, you are doing your marriage a favor if you look young, and up-to-date. That doesn't mean you try to squeeze into teenage styles two sizes too small for you! But you can choose fashionable, young-looking clothes that are appropriate for you. Above all avoid looking like your mother!!

If you are wearing fashionable clothes, you will have more self-confidence and carry yourself with more poise. When you feel better about yourself, you are free to care about others and not be self-centered. Your confidence also shows that you have chosen your clothes with care. Once you have put them on and made sure everything is in place, you can forget yourself. Have you noticed that you are more concerned with yourself when you are wearing something which doesn't fit, or in which you feel dowdy or out of place? You are less free to concentrate on others because you are preoccupied with your appearance.

Wearing fashionable clothing styles lets your husband and others know that you are not behind the times. Being "out of date" in your physical appearance, and in your thinking, is thought of as being "old" and "dull." Your husband and other people will feel that your thinking is up-to-date if you're keeping current with today's clothing styles.

Of course, it would be poor stewardship to change your entire wardrobe with every passing fad. Also avoid fashions if they are not right for your figure. If you choose more classical styles, you will be able to wear them for more years. You might use a basic suit for years, but you can continually update it with a current blouse, scarf, or jewelry.

TOPPING IT OFF

The hairstyle you choose should not be dictated by fashion unless it is right for you. Many midlife women latch onto a short hairstyle, whether or not it looks good on them, because it is easy to maintain.

Midlife women often choose a short haircut because "hot flashes" and a busy life-style make it hard to care for longer, curly hair. Your hairstyle needs to be the most complimentary one for you. Don't feel pressured to wear your hair according to the latest fad, nor to look as if you're ten years behind current styles.

Many men like longer hair on women, but certainly not all men. Learn which way your husband prefers and wear it to please him. At the same time consider your facial shape, body size, hair texture, and so on. Find a hairstylist who will work with you in finding a suitable style, and if you don't plan on going to the hairdresser frequently, have the stylist show you how to fix your hair yourself.

EMPHASIZING THE POSITIVE

Long ago I (Sally) heard the following little poem derisively chanted:

> A little bit of powder
> And a little bit of paint
> Often make a woman
> Look like what she ain't!

Do you know people who feel that using makeup is wrong? "If God had meant for you to have bright red lips, he would have made them that way." That same philosophy could be carried so far as to say, "If God had meant for you to have short fingernails, he wouldn't cause them to grow." (I don't even know any Bible verse that supports the practice of keeping our nails trimmed!) Or, how about, "If God had intended for you to wear clothes, he would have had you born covered."

Of course, using makeup in excess and taking an inordinate amount of time to apply it is wrong, just as anything in excess is wrong. Maximizing your good features and minimizing your poorer ones, however, is a part of good stewardship. If you apply the same principle in the area of your talents, you would do the things that you are most able to do well and not take time doing those for which you are ungifted.

For example, it would be a waste of my (Sally) time to be a church pianist. I reached the limit of my musical ability at a low level. I have other abilities, however, and I exercise those. We don't criticize people for doing what they are most gifted to do. Shouldn't we have the same attitude about our physical assets?

I know a friendly, perky, shapely girl with beautiful hair and a lovely smile. Unfortunately, she has a nose that is too large for the rest of her features. She has learned to add just the right touch of makeup in the right places to give the allusion of having a smaller nose. As a result, she is a beautiful girl, and I don't call that hypocritical – at least, no more so than for the woman who chooses clothing that doesn't accentuate her large hips.

The opposite of no makeup, of course, is too much makeup or poorly applied makeup. I think of Alice. The first time I saw her with her wig askew, her artificial eyelashes slipping, her eyebrows crooked, and her lipstick smeared, I thought, "She must have had to hurry to get dressed this morning. Or maybe the lighting over her mirror was poor." But the next time I saw her she looked the same. Then I thought, "She's doing it for a joke. She wants to see if someone will say something." I wasn't going to be that someone! I saw her several times and she always looked as if she had just had a fight with a giant propeller with a dripping paintbrush attached to it. Her appearance distracted me so much that I had trouble seeing her positive qualities.

Men like makeup if they don't know you have it on – or if at least you don't look painted. The secret is using enough of the right makeup in the right places is to make you look like a natural beauty!

THE FEMININE MYSTIQUE

Another asset for beauty which you possess is your femininity. Sadly, some people who push women's rights, have felt that femininity is sexist and a deceitful ploy to keep women as second-class citizens.

We believe in the equality of men and women, but we don't see equality as removing the gender of women, or making women feel as if their femininity is somehow beneath them. We cannot deny that God created two different sexes and that he gave them different physical characteristics. The outrage has come when ungodly cultures have treated the two sexes differently. And a further outrage has been committed when, in the name of Christianity, our church fathers (and recently a few mothers) have perpetuated this difference.

BIBLICAL EQUALITY

If you could completely forget what sex you happened to be born and look without any prejudice at the original language of the Bible, you would see that God intends men and women to be equal in position, authority, responsibility, in submission, and as heirs together of God's grace. God created both in his image and gave them both authority over creation (Genesis 2:26-28). They both sinned and they both had consequences to pay (Genesis 3). They each have responsibilities to the other as husband and wife (1 Corinthians 7:3-5; Ephesians 5:21-33). Christ's example in the Gospels is the ultimate in showing that God intended men and women to be equal.

And even those tricky passages in the Epistles, such as those in which women are commanded to keep silent in church and not to teach, can be understood when you know that the issue is fidelity to marriage, rather than church leadership roles. For a detailed study on a woman's position in God's sight, we suggest you look at the Internet for books which discuss husband-and-wife equality from a Christian point of view.

The point I want to make is that you should be true to your sexuality. As an overreaction to the exploitation of women, some have tried to extinguish their sex difference by unisex clothing and hairstyles. Being equal *doesn't* mean you have to look the same or hold the same jobs. Being equal *does* mean that if you hold the same job you should get the same pay. Being true to your sexuality means you are free to be the feminine person God created.

You do not have to compete with males to prove your worth. You are part of God's creative order because you are female – your husband is also part of God's plan because he is male. Sexuality is the very essence of your personhood.

GLAD TO BE FEMININE

Human sexuality is more than just our sexual anatomical differences, or having an orgasm, or the ability to reproduce children. Human sexuality gives us the ability to contribute to each other from a different point of view. Human sexuality provides us the opportunity to give and receive intimacy, love, affirmation, and caring. Release of sexual tension is a part of human sexuality, but far more we are enabled to enrich another's life.

When you accept your sexuality, you are moving toward the acceptance of yourself as a total person. We have said that self-acceptance is a key to a good self-image, and a good self-image is a key to accepting and loving others. When you accept your femininity, you are closer to peace with yourself. Then you are free to provide for your husband's physical and emotional needs.

Ingrid Trobisch in *The Joy of Being a Woman* says, "Living and accepting one's own gender is the greatest help which the sexes' can give to each other. I cannot accept my partner unless I accept myself. I cannot love my partner unless I love myself."[5] Mrs. Trobisch challenges us to accept the difficult physical aspects of our being female – our menstrual cycle and childbirth – to "live in harmony" with every part of ourselves.

Why all this talk about being feminine in a chapter on physical health and appearance? If you accept your sexuality, you will enjoy being a woman. This will influence how you care for your body and your physical appearance. Looking great and feeling good will help you and your husband during this crucial time of midlife.

> **Thank you for making me so wonderfully complex! Your workmanship is marvelous – and how well I know it. You watched me as I was being formed in the utter seclusion, as I was woven together in the dark of the womb. You saw me before I was born. Every day of my life was recorded in your book. Every moment was laid out before a single day had passed. (Psalms 139:14-16)**

Now we want to talk about additional ways you can help your husband survive his midlife crisis.

(A note from Jim: After a 7 year battle, Sally died from breast cancer. Sally went through massive rounds

of chemotherapy, radiation, plus she had 3 surgeries. We often asked ourselves why this happened – why would such a talented, witty, intelligent, spiritual, and gifted woman be taken out of the world? Could we have lived differently to reduce the possibility of cancer?

Second guessing is always difficult – but we do know that we lived under lots of stress from my dysfunctional family, and from our intense ministry life-style. Also Sally didn't want to bother with the daily breast exams – until her lump was the size of a golf ball. By then over half of her lymph nodes were malignant. So don't forget take care of the body God has given you!)

Part four
HELPING YOUR HUSBAND

15

WINNING ATTITUDES

Fran was a midlife woman who suddenly realized her forty-something husband was doing things that were quite unlike him. She realized that he had been behaving strangely for several months, but at first she thought little about it. Now she was painfully aware that something was really wrong.

Fran's husband, Ray, was a professional man who was very devoted to his family. He was a leader in his church. He was a humble, unselfish person, and people thought highly of him. He had never been a talker, but when he spoke, he was worth listening to.

Now he was often withdrawn, sometimes sullen, and even filled with self-pity around home. In public he made the effort to appear friendly, but the stress of putting on a front, when he felt lousy, became so difficult that he began to find excuses not to attend church and community functions. He became angry and grumpy. He started working more hours and coming home later than he said he would. Then he began calling to say he wasn't coming home at all some evenings. He wanted to be alone to think.

That's when Fran was jolted into reality. But reality stung. She hurt so much that she eventually sought help from her pastor. Her pastor helped her to see that Ray was in midlife transition with many things weighing on his mind – causing him terrific pressure. Fran began to read as much as she could about this period in life so that she could understand Ray. Then she did all she could to help him. The two of them had some rough times for many months.

Ray confessed that for the first time in his married life he was seriously considering another woman. She was younger and he had shared some of his concerns with her – when Fran hadn't seemed to care. He hadn't meant to get so emotionally involved, and even though they weren't sexually involved, Ray felt he loved the other woman.

Ray made it successfully through his midlife crisis without leaving Fran and without leaving his profession. Fran stuck with him through thick and thin. They learned to communicate more honestly and to be more alert to each other's needs. Today their marriage is stronger than ever.

When you started to read this story, you might have thought we were talking about you and your husband. Sally and I have heard similar stories from hundreds of midlife women. The above account is basically about one couple, whose names have been changed, but the situation fits many midlife couples today.

ENOUGH IS TOO MUCH

Not all stories end happily. Sue and Pete are a typical

example. Pete's midlife trauma also caught Sue off guard. They were intelligent, friendly, and spiritual people. His profession brought him in touch with many interesting job opportunities. Sue was also a growing, fascinating, and attractive person. But she absolutely did not understand the turmoil Pete was telling her about. He had always been so sure of himself and his philosophy of life. Why was he questioning and doubting his beliefs and values now?

Sue kept busy with the children and her part-time career – and didn't let Pete's troubles bother her. When he finally told her he was spending time with a young woman, she exploded. That was enough! She told him to leave and not come back until he quit the affair! When he continued to be confused for some weeks and was living with the third in a series of women, Sue quickly filed for divorce. She was convinced he had permanently changed. She hastily remarried and soon realized she had made a poor choice for a second husband, but was stuck.

Then Pete contacted her to say he seemed to have his head on straight once more and for the past few months had been feeling like himself again. Would there be a chance of restoring their marriage and reuniting the family? But it was too late.

Not all midlife marriages are saved or broken because of the wife. But during a husband's midlife crisis, the wife is a big factor in whether or not the relationship will survive.

MORE THAN SURVIVAL

The early chapters of this book tell you something about a man's midlife problems. Perhaps you've done some additional reading in *Men in Midlife Crisis, or When a Mate Wants Out,* or other books we have mentioned. We've looked at the problems your husband's trauma causes you and some ways you can be strengthened. This next part of the book is aimed at giving practical suggestions – so you can help your husband survive. Hopefully, both of you will be more than mere survivors. We pray that together you will be triumphant winners!

Your attitudes can have a major impact to make or break your husband. When you realize your husband is entering his midlife transition, or if you want to be prepared for that time, decide now which attitudes will rule you. Rededicate yourself each day – perhaps many times each day. And remember, you cannot keep your vows to have positive attitudes by your own strength. You will get tired, become selfish, and short-sighted. You need Christ's power in you every moment. Apply Philippians 4:13 to your situation, "For I can do everything through Christ who gives me strength."

THE COMMITMENT COST

The first attitude you need is commitment. Commit yourself to your marriage – and to your husband as a man. The major question to ask is, "Do I want to keep this marriage?" Unless you really want to stay in the marriage, you will probably not be able to live with all the stress and sacrifice you will make over the next three to five years. If you are committed to your marriage, decide to do everything within your power to keep and improve your relationship, and to support, build, and love your husband.

This commitment means that many times you will have to put your own needs and desires aside and zero in on his. This may be the hundredth time you've done so this week! But by God's strength, you are going to do it again – and again.

Commit yourself to the art of understanding your husband. Specialize in knowing what your husband thinks, feels, values, worries over, plus his fears about the future. Learn what pleases him, how he views himself – everything that makes him what he is.

Then *commit* yourself to accept him just as he is right now and to help him close the gaps he senses in his life. You are not to decide what you think his needs are, but you have to meet the needs *he is feeling*. For example, he may be complaining that he never gets enough leisure time. You might be tempted to point out all the hours he has spent watching television this week (hours that you didn't get because you were busy with the children and the house!). But He feels that he hasn't had enough leisure time. You can help him think through things he might do to feel he is getting recreation, and then urge him to actually do those activities.

Sometimes women will strongly react at this point saying, "What about my needs??" We will deal with your legitimate needs later – and your needs are legitimate!!

But for this time in your lives *commit* yourself to stick by him for as long as it takes to get him through this midlife transition. How long that will be depends upon the individual situation – your husband's self-knowledge, plus his self-esteem, job satisfaction, marriage satisfaction, and physical health. Additional factors are your understanding and help, his relationship with his children, and a whole lot of other factors. The total midlife transition takes years, but the actual crisis period may take from several months to a few years.

CAN I HOLD ON?

Midlife crisis is not like the flu. A man doesn't have it for a few days and get over it. From our experience in counseling hundreds of midlife couples over a period of 25 years, we have concluded that the unsettled period seems to average about 3 years, with a gradual beginning for some months, then several months or a year of acute stress, and a gradual improvement for some more months. When a midlife woman first asks for help in coping with her husband's strange behavior, we ask her to commit to living with the situation for as long as 3 to 5 years.

Don't let the time overwhelm you. You only have to live one day at a time! The midlife crisis is a developmental process, and it takes time – the same as adolescence takes time. When your child turns 13, you don't have to live the next 5 to 7 years all at one time. You go from one day to the next until that child has arrived at the end of the teen developmental time. Your child is passing from being a child to being an adult. You have good times and bad, but hopefully, you and your teens have both learned a lot, and have grown closer to each other. Adolescence is normal (but that doesn't mean painless!). So is your husband's midlife transition.

LOVE IS SAYING YOU'RE SORRY

Once you have committed yourself to helping your husband – what's next? There are more helpful attitudes you will need. "But," you say, "I thought I worked on myself enough in the last few chapters. When do I start working on my husband?"

Let's start by confession of sin – not your husband's, but yours. "But he's the one who has been acting like a rat. He should ask me to forgive him!" you sputter.

A key to midlife marriage restoration is your willingness to recognize that you are a part of the dissatisfaction. True, he is the other part. But for now focus on your contribution to the marriage troubles. Confess your failure, weakness, stubbornness, insensitivity, and other faults which have undermined your marriage. Tell God you are sorry – and tell your husband. Your genuine contrition for having wronged your husband is necessary for your wholeness, whether or not your husband ever sees his errors, and whether or not he ever forgives you for yours. God promises forgiveness and to let you start over clean. "But if we confess our sins to Him, He is faithful and just to forgive us our sins and to cleanse us from all wickedness" (1 John 1:9).

HE HASN'T CONFESSED

Closely related to your asking to be forgiven, is *forgiving your husband*. "Wait a minute!" you protest. "I've gone out on a limb to confess my wrongs in the relationship. Now you're asking me to forgive him for his part – but he hasn't even said he's sorry. Besides that, he doesn't think he's done anything wrong. Everything's my fault in his eyes."

One of the most helpful things you can do for your husband is to free him so he can change. You do this by forgiving him for all the ways in which he has offended you – even if he doesn't ask to be forgiven.

Two things happen when you forgive your husband. First, you are set free so that the problem is not eating you. When you turn over your role as judge to God, you complete your responsibility to make sure your husband confesses his wrongs. Second, as you forgive your husband, he is again assured that God will forgive him. He senses that if a mere human can genuinely forgive him, and then certainly a loving God will forgive and restore him too.

HELPING GOD

It is not your place to punish your husband, or make him feel guilty. Some of our midlife friends keep asking us, "Do you think my husband feels guilty about what he is doing? Do you think he realizes how wrong he is?" His sensitivity to sin is God's responsibility. Your task is to forgive him and love him.

To forgive is not to forget. Nor is it pretending the offenses never occurred. Forgiveness is not an emotional response. It doesn't demand the offending party change before we forgive. Most of all, forgiveness is not easy.

Grab this phrase, "To forgive is not to forget." I (Sally) have always been told that true forgiveness means totally forgetting, and yet I could never completely forget some incidents in my life.

I (Jim) also have struggled with a meaning of forgiveness. I was raised in a dysfunctional family where there were many emotionally and spiritually destructive things going on. My father had repeated affairs with other women – and he treated my mother with great disrespect. Additionally, there were a number of times when my brother and I were beaten very severely – way beyond what our offense warranted.

Frequently, throughout my adult life, I would tell God that I was forgiving my father – even though he never did ask forgiveness for what he did, nor even offer any expression of sorrow for these events.

My continued problem was that, "If I had truly forgiven my father, then I would not remember the events." But through "prayer therapy" I have come to experience God's healing as He took away the pain of the memory – even though I can fully recall those evil events.

Those events are all now just history in my mind – the same way that I have read about graphic, and bloody, events of the American Civil War. But those are just the events – without any pain attached. So I have forgiven my father – it is history – and it no longer turns my stomach. Forgiveness has relieved the pain of the memory.

LOVE WITHOUT STRINGS
An attitude that follows forgiveness is *love*. You might not agree that love is an attitude if you think love is something you fall in or out of. Falling in and out of love is based on feelings. To identify love with a feeling is fatal, because feelings change. Feelings are fickle. However, it is also fatal to deny warmth and loving words and actions to your spouse, because loving words and actions help your love to flourish.

Loving your husband includes accepting him as he is at this moment. When you love your husband, you value him without strings attached. You don't say, "When he changes, I will love him," or, "If he will do thus and so, I can give myself to this relationship again." Unconditional love may not be your natural response to your husband at this time, but you can work at it. Since love is more than a feeling that simply happens without your control – it involves your will, and you can work at building your will to love.

Love grows by cultivation, by looking at the positive qualities of the one you love, and by putting yourself out to meet his needs. Contempt and hate grow by cultivation too – by looking at the negative qualities and actions of the other one, by selfishly not doing the kind of things that help him. You can use your will to decide whether to love, or to despise your husband.

YOUR WAY – OR HIS?

When you show love to your husband, do it in a way that is meaningful to him. He may not care at all that you are using a special tablecloth, flowers, and candlelight for dinner – but you may think he is really going to know you love him by your extra effort. However, he might prefer that you take time to watch a football game with him. He may not be convinced you love him by the special cards and notes as much as by your withholding criticism when he doesn't get around to washing the car.

Bruce Larson tells a wonderful story of the parents who learned to show love in a meaningful way to their teenage sons who were disappointing them very much – because of the tough friends they chose to hang out with. The boys skipped the church youth programs to do things with the motorcycle friends. There was a growing barrier between the parents and their sons.

Mom suddenly realized she could show the tremendous love she felt for her boys, by accepting and loving their friends. She invited their tough friends to their home and made them feel welcome. As a result, the relationship between the parents and sons was transformed, and eventually the leader of the gang came to know Christ. Perhaps you can think of creative ways to express your love to your husband in a way he can understand – meeting his needs, not yours.

You can show your husband you love him by adopting a "no nag" policy, by not manipulating him with tears, sex, or other means – and by affirming and encouraging him. The way love behaves is expressed in 1 Corinthians 13, "Love is patient and kind. Love is not jealous or boastful or proud or rude. It does not demand its own way. It is not irritable, and it keeps no record of being wronged. It does not rejoice about injustice but rejoices whenever the truth wins out. Love never gives up, never loses faith, is always hopeful, and endures through every circumstance" (1 Corinthians 13:4-7).

Sometimes when I (Sally) started to be irritated about something Jim did which displease me, I remember, "Love covers all transgressions" (Proverbs 10:12) or, "Love forgets mistakes" (Proverbs 17: 9). Often there's no better way to handle an offense than to cover it with your love and forgive the offender. That doesn't mean that you cease to be assertive – when assertiveness is needed. But most of us need more practice in forgiving and loving, than we do in sticking up for our rights.

TUNE IN
Another helpful attitude during your husband's midlife crisis is *alertness*. Many wives are totally unaware of the stresses their husbands are undergoing until they reach the traumatic stage. If you are aware of the signs at the very start of his midlife transition, you can help minimize some of the problems. If he seems depressed, encourage him to talk. You may learn that he is beginning to feel threatened at work. He may not express that fear, however, unless you let him know you are an ally, wanting to listen to his concerns. When he does talk over his worries and feelings, be sure to empathize. Don't ridicule, criticize, or advise him. Don't give pat answers. Listen and encourage him.

Many wives don't know when their husbands are depressed or discouraged because they aren't paying any attention. You may have many valid reasons for your insensitivity – busy career, children, social obligations, or just plain thoughtlessness – but the results of insensitivity are always negative.

Your husband may not be asking for your attention, but that isn't good either. Not being aware of your "hurting husband" or if he isn't looking to you for help, indicates you are drifting apart in your care and concern for each other. Work to close the gap. Cultivate these characteristics – asking, listening, empathizing, remembering, being tender, seeing, comforting, touching, and hanging out together.

THE FLEXIBLE FRAU

Another state of mind that will be valuable during your husband's midlife crisis is actually a pair of attitudes "flexibility" and "availability." By this time in your marriage, you may have grown accustomed to living your own life and keeping your own schedule – while your husband has been busy with his career. You may have a set pattern for how daily life is to run.

Then your husband begins to act discontented and wants something different. He may start hobbies and other interests for which he never took time before. He may want you to join him in these new activities, and you'll be wise if you do. He may want more time talking with you. There certainly will be changes in his life-style, and you need to be ready to bend.

You should be available to him more than you ever have been before. That may mean you leave the kids with a baby-sitter, or on their own while you go away with him for a weekend. Surprise yourself by attending sports equipment shows with him. You may have aching muscles you never knew you had as you take up biking. For me (Sally), one of the changes was sailing with Jim on his newly acquired "Midlife Crisis sailboat." I'm not a natural-born sailor as he is, and relaxation for me is not dodging the boom – as we tacked back and forth across the undersized lakes in Illinois. But I was determined to enjoy sailing anyway – because I wanted to be with Jim!

LIFE-STYLE REVIEW

There may be other life-style changes. For some women, it may be dressing to please him, or changing a hairstyle. It may be developing a carefree attitude so that you are more fun. It could be making yourself more available for sex with your husband.

Some women object to making changes. They feel they are denying their true selves. Keep your goal in perspective! Right now, you want to help your husband successfully navigate his midlife transition – including marriage improvement and your personal growth and change. You probably will discover that most of the changes your husband needs will also please you.

One of the life-style changes I (Sally) made was to resign from teaching. I had returned to teaching part-time to help pay college tuition when Barbara and Brenda chose to attend a private Christian college. Then one year I had to accept a full-time position if I wanted to keep my job.

That was the year Jim went headlong into his midlife crisis. One of his problems was lack of sufficient rest and relaxation because of the 80 to 100 hour weeks he worked as pastor of our active church. He had previously taken Mondays as his day off

– but he felt guilty about relaxing a whole day while I was away working.

Because I was gone from home longer each day, my housework had to be crammed into a shorter time. I had less time for Jim if he was home in the evening. Because I needed enough rest to keep up with my students for a full day, I became very rigid about getting to sleep by a certain time each night. Our stressed schedules often left no quiet, relaxing moments in bed to chat casually.

That spring I began to sense that Jim needed more from me than I could give him when I was teaching full-time. Still, we certainly needed the income and I was enjoying success in my profession.

God did two things for me to help me make a decision. One was a growing discontentment with my work. There wasn't any good explanation. I was still successful, I still loved my students, and I enjoyed my colleagues. But I could hardly stand every half-hour of each day. I think that feeling was necessary to help me cut ties.

God also used Proverbs 31:16 to convince me that for now my place was at home – so I could better provide for Jim's needs. That verse convinced me that at this time I needed to be caring for my vineyard at home – my husband.

I still had a struggle when the time actually came to submit my resignation because of pressure from others in the profession. It was hard for them to believe I was simply going to stay home and work on projects with my husband. Yet I experienced complete peace about my decision.

My expanded time at home enabled me to work with Jim doing research, editing, and typing of our first book, *Men in Midlife Crisis.* I was also free to participate with him at conferences and seminars. Any loss I experienced when I left my teaching position was more than repaid by the reward and fulfillment of my new speaking and writing career with Jim.

BEYOND STAGNATION

One more attitude to cultivate during your husband's midlife crisis is that of *determining to grow spiritually, emotionally, intellectually*, or in whatever way God leads you. You will be a better person, plus many midlife men reject anything that hints of being "old." If you are stagnant in your personal growth, you may appear "old" to him.

What are you doing to learn more about local, national and world affairs? Today's woman can't afford to be uninformed. What goals have you set for this next year? Perhaps you plan to study the current philosophies of womanhood and compare them to Christian principles and decide what you believe. Perhaps this is the time to enroll in that upholstering class. Have you taken Red Cross CPR lessons (cardiopulmonary resuscitation) so you might help save someone's life? Your husband, remember, is in the heart-attack period of his life!

Perhaps you have evaluated your time commitments, and right now you aren't going to take on any additional outside activities. You can still be a growing person by keeping your daily reflection time God, taking another 15 minutes sometime during the day to read from a book to stretch your vision, and listening to a daily news broadcast. You may say you don't have time to read books, and so you just don't get started. But 15 minutes a day with 30 minutes on Sunday adds up to 2 hours a week – or about 12 to 15 books a year. It's better to read a little bit regularly than to wait for a big block of time which may never come.

BUT HE'S MINE!

Perhaps one of the hardest attitudes to maintain during your husband's midlife crisis will be *relinquishment.* You are doing all this stuff – praising him, listening, understanding his needs, praying for him, and doing your best to improve yourself and your marriage, yet you also have to surrender any claim you might have on him. He still has his own will. You do not possess him.

On the one hand, you need to do all you can to help him, yet allow him independence. That doesn't mean you throw up your hands and yell, "Go, do whatever you want! I don't care!" It does mean that you quietly acknowledge his right to himself. It's easier to relax your grasp if you commit him to God. The Holy Spirit will do a much more effective job of building his inner man than you can by your possessiveness.

"Wow! Getting through this ordeal sure gets complicated," you say in despair. We know. We've been there. And so have lots of other women – but it is God who gives us the peace and rest we need.

> **Unless the Lord builds the house, the work of the builders is useless. Unless the Lord protects the city, guarding it with sentries will do no good.**

It is useless for you to work so hard from early morning until late at night, anxiously working for food to eat; for God gives rest to his loved ones. (Psalms 127:1-2)

In the next chapter let's focus on understanding and meeting your special guy's needs.

16

UNDERSTANDING HIS NEEDS

To start, get informed about this midlife period of his life. You can't assume you know what his needs are if you don't know about the unique stresses of midlife. Midlife involves extreme battles within your man and the world around him. A midlife man questions every aspect of his life, and often times, he is confused, depressed, angry, and sometimes horrified by what he sees. He blames himself, and others, for his real or imagined failures. He cannot live life as usual, but needs time to choose a new path, or alter the old one.

Jim changed so very much during his midlife crisis. He would sit in the living room chair, staring out the large picture window, as if he was in a trance and unable to move. This was very unusual for Jim because he usually started his day about 6 AM, and would move through the day like a human tornado dealing with all of the issues related to a large growing church – not stopping until he dropped into bed about 11 PM.

Relax! Allow this struggle to take place. Midlife is a normal developmental period, and your husband is working on normal midlife tasks. He has a need to question and evaluate his life. As strange, and as difficult as it may seem, he is going through an extremely healthy process. Our goal is to try and help him make the best use of this midlife evaluation process. You can be a sounding board for his questioning if you know it's profitable for him. If you don't, you are likely to get anxious, or turn him off, so he doesn't share his search with you.

TEMPORARY TURBULENCE

You can be encouraged by knowing that this tumultuous time is temporary. Many women, who have *not* known about the midlife crisis, have become fearful when their husbands begin to behave strangely. Some women think their husbands are going to be this way the rest of their lives. Women have hurried into a divorce, thinking, "He isn't the man I married, and I'm not going to put up with him."

This midlife transition is a normal and necessary stage in life. This limited upheaval will pass. If the midlife man does not make unwise decisions during his crisis, life on the other side will be much calmer. Men who make rash work changes, divorce their wives, or run away, have more complications to work out after their inner struggle has quieted down. If both husband and wife can see that the midlife crisis period is temporary, they will have the courage to hang on during the rough times.

You may not know it, but one of the big fears men face during midlife is the feeling they are failing at everything. If superiors or colleagues are unhappy with them at work, they feel deficient. If they are unhappy with their type of occupation, they blame themselves for the poor choice they made.

If you are unhappy with your husband, he feels he is failing you. If he is unhappy with you, he again feels it's his fault for selecting the wrong mate. If the kids are rebellious, he feels he has failed as a father. If he is overcommitted at church or in the community, he feels he is stupid for getting so involved. If he isn't doing anything for church or community, he sees himself as not carrying his load. No matter what he is or isn't doing, his gloomy view of himself is seen as his personal failure. He may not voice this feeling loudly enough so you can discuss it openly, but if you are alert to his dismal view of himself, you can do and say positive things to give him assurance of his worth.

A missionary acquaintance, from Asia, was doing a fantastically successful job of evangelism, training leaders, and leadership for his mission. In his early 40s, he began to feel frustrated with his growing inability to keep doing all he was doing. He didn't have the strength he used to have, and he worried that life was running out too fast for all he needed to do.

His wife felt he was never around and that their marriage lacked the fun and spontaneity of the early years. One of their teenage boys also felt left out. He got involved in drugs and started hanging out with a tough group of people – and declared himself not to be a Christian.

It became a strange irony – the parents were missionaries trying to win people to Jesus in Asia – while the son declared himself an atheist, and was living a very pagan life-style.

Sadly, the son became overwhelmed with guilt and shame. He felt trapped – so trapped that he felt the only solution was to take his life. The boy's decision caused such trauma in the family, that the very successful missionary father also killed himself. This midlife father reasoned that he had failed his son, his wife, his missionary organization, and ultimately God – he also felt hopeless, and ended his life.

Don't let the midlife era panic you into making some rash decisions! Remember, this is just a developmental life stage – and life is going to get better!

ONE MORE LOOK

During part of the crisis your husband may have an urge to go back to earlier days. Sometimes the "going back" may be an attempt to make up for disappointments in earlier relationships. If he did not get along well with a family member during his teens or 20s, he may now try to strengthen the ties. The past years he may have been too busy to keep in touch with his school friends, or relatives. Now he seems to need to reestablish old communication lines, to get a look at them again, and learn where they are in their lives.

He may hardly have looked at the invitation for his tenth class reunion, but when it is time for the twentieth, he will go to any length to get there. He may spend hoarded money, or go several hours out of his way on a business trip to look up an "old friend." He may want to visit the area in which he spent the most memorable time of his childhood. This is all part of the process of looking back over the territory he has covered in his life – before he starts out across a new frontier.

One of the reasons it is hard to meet your husband's needs during this time is because he vacillates in what he wants – and about what pleases him. Just when you think you have figured out what to do, he wants something different. Sometimes he wants you to mother him – at other times he will resent it. At times he wants you to be his carefree lover – other times he wants you to be a responsible mother/wife. Of course, we all have mood changes from time to time, but a midlife man often has extremely wide mood swings. This time is very unsettled and frustrating for him. If you can be resilient with his vacillating moods, you can cushion some of the rocky times.

EVERYTHING STINKS

A major emotion your husband may display is anger. He is angry that he is getting older, angry he feels tired, angry that his financial obligations are grinding him under, angry he hasn't reached his career goals – or that he has and it hasn't made happy. He is angry that life is a big waste of time, angry that you don't understand him, or do what pleases him. He is also angry that the kids only want him for the things he can provide, angry that no one appreciates him, angry that God has let life be this way. He is Angry, Angry, *ANGRY*! When his anger isn't erupting, he sits depressed with his negative emotions boiling inside.

Let your husband know that it's all right to feel angry. Admitting he has those feelings is one step toward healing. He doesn't need to feel guilty about having feelings. Remember that anger is not sinful, it's just a feeling. All physical, emotional, and psychological feelings are normal. So are the temptations which arise from these natural feelings. No one needs to feel guilty about the natural parts of themselves. Anger usually is the result of feeling a loss, rejection, or frustration. What we do with the anger we feel is the real issue. Anger does have the positive ability to push us into action. Pray that your guy will not choose evil, but use his anger for growth and health.

If you can keep your cool and are objective, you can let your husband spill his angry feelings out to you. That doesn't mean you should let him physically or verbally attack you. But you can help dissipate his anger by listening. Stay calm and don't inflame your husband's feelings. If you can be an objective listener, you will be vital in helping him get over his anger – and get on to constructive actions. And most of all remember that logical arguing with him will not help at all!

OTHER HELPERS

In other sections we have talked about the importance of temporarily putting aside your own needs, accepting your husband as he is, developing sensitivity and empathy, and giving lots of affirmation. You can also enlist outside help. You don't have to start a huge campaign of "Help my pathetic husband." You can, however, promote natural contacts with friends who will be an encouragement and stimulation for him.

You can tactfully involve your adult children, relatives and friends in ways which will affirm him. Since our book, *Men in Midlife Crisis* was published, many leaders have started classes or small groups for midlife men, or couples, to learn and get mutual strength from each other. It would be great if every church, hospital, and adult education program would provide classes or retreats to help midlife people.

Encourage your husband to find suitable outlets for his new desires to connect or change his life. Many men feel a compulsion to withdraw from everything. Help your husband find times when he really can withdraw from all responsibilities. He probably won't be able to do that for long periods, or very often, but if he has a definite time set aside when he can do as he wants, without meeting any obligations, this will help.

Often he will feel a little better for a short time and then may feel the urge to withdraw again. Help him get mini-retreats. He may want to spend an evening watching television without any interruptions – or without any family members watching with him, or he may want to go for a long walk by himself. He may want to call an old buddy, skip a few days at work, putter with his hobby, or just skip a meeting. It is better that he drop out for short periods, than to hang on until he completely snaps and drops out permanently.

THE RUNAWAY

Another strong pull many men feel is to run away – escape from all their pressures. Again, it is better for a man to have small, appropriate escape times than to be forced into disappearing completely, and permanently, in order to find relief. I (Jim) found it helpful to get into the car and drive and drive – with no destination in mind. Sometimes I found relief by biking for miles in the country. Other times I would take an afternoon for sailing. Once in a while Sally and I went camping for 2 or 3 days. Before this, we had never gone away except for a week or two during our official vacation time. I found it necessary, during my midlife crisis, to take many short breaks between our annual vacations. The short breaks provided a temporary relief so I could hold on again for a while.

SAILBOAT OR MINI COOPER

Buying my sailboat was another way I allowed myself a suitable outlet for some of my confusing feelings. Many men have sacrificed for their families for years – but during midlife they begin to spend money lavishly on themselves. Some have never had the sports car, ski equipment, or the boat they wanted. Sadly some men go into tremendous debt for these personal luxuries. They become obsessed with the need to make up for deprivation they've felt.

I (Sally) knew Jim's growing desire to sail and to have his own boat, so I encouraged him to get one. About this time, Jim had been passing out at the office, and we had spent hundreds of dollars on medical tests only to learn that these spells were caused by exhaustion. I decided the money would be better spent on a boat to give him the recreation he needed – so I encouraged Jim to get a sailboat. Within days he had found just the perfect used 16' HobieCat sailboat, at a great price.

(Note: I still have that sailboat on a lake in Northern Michigan where I now live, and our grandkids, my wife Jan and I, have been able to have lots of fun with it.)

Encourage your husband to find appropriate releases from his pressures so he doesn't have to do something extreme to meet his needs. He may not get long breaks, or get them frequently, but help him get mini-vacations. He may not get to own a Porsche, but perhaps your next car could be more fun to drive. Simply knowing that you understand his changing needs will relieve some of the pressure for him.

A FRIEND INDEED

Being his best friend will be a valuable asset for both of you during this time. You have many roles to perform – wife, homemaker, lover, and co-parent. But being his best friend is more important than all the rest.

What does a best friend do? Listens, encourages, stimulates, gives insight, is loyal, is available at all times, goes places with him, is interested in his work, shares his hobbies – and knows when to sit in silence.

You have the advantage of being able to prove you are a true friend because you know the most about your husband, including his weaknesses, and you remain loyal and caring. You have been with him through the years, watching him grow and develop, and you can appreciate what he has put into becoming what he is now. Others may admire him when he is doing well and when he can do something for them – but you are the *one person* in the world who can see his worth and stick with him when he is sour, ugly, and broken. You may be helped during this time by reading another of our books titled, *When A Mate Wants Out.*[1]

Your enabling power by being his best friend will not happen because you have some great reservoir of goodness in you. It must be the power of God flowing through your life. Your own strength will run out, and your own needs will cry for attention. You will have to rely on Christ.

Try to imagine how Christ would love your husband. Jesus would listen to him, be patient, encourage, give your husband perspective and hope – yes and even give him the important prod to keep growing to be the man your guy wants to be. Jesus gives us a practical example to follow. Plus we have this promise, "And the Lord – who is the Spirit – makes us more and more like him as we are changed into his glorious image" (2 Corinthians 3:18b).

As you allow God to work in you, your response to your husband will be more and more like Christ's response. You will then be in a position to help your husband work through his troublesome midlife development, so that both of you are winners.

> **My heart is breaking as I remember how it used to be. I walked among the crowds of worshipers . . . singing for joy and giving thanks. Why am I discouraged? Why am I sad? I will put my hope in God! I will praise him again – my Savior and my God! (Psalms 42:4, 5a)**

17

HELPING HIM WIN

Our friend Dick, a small-business owner, had experienced a few ups and downs in his life. But now he had been down for many months. He didn't feel there were any more ups left for him. When he and Rita were first married he owned and operated his own small business, which had been moderately successful. Five years ago he joined a large retail firm in the same line of business. At first he was praised for his contributions to the company and was given promotions in the early years. Now, however, his superiors and colleagues were increasingly on his back to produce more, and to work longer hours. There were even hints that a younger man, recently hired, might get his job.

Three years ago Rita had started a part-time job, working five mornings a week. She still took care of the home, taught a Sunday school class, led a Bible study in her home every Thursday afternoon, was program chairman for the community women's group, and was co-president with her husband of the married couple's fellowship of their church.

Wouldn't the couple's fellowship be surprised if they knew

how bad things really were between them at home! Rita had become short-tempered and impatient with everyone in the family. Dick wished she weren't so devoted to her morning job, so she'd be less tense at home. But then, she had always been easily upset if things didn't go her way.

He began to have trouble remembering what had ever attracted him to her. Maybe it was a mistake to get married to her in the first place. They certainly didn't have much in common any more. She didn't seem to care that he was having trouble at work. All she was interested in was getting to her job on time, having the house clean, and being prepared for teaching and leading her groups – he didn't seem to count.

FAILING FATHER

Three of their four children had left home. When the kids were younger, Dick would have said he had a close relationship with his kids, but now there seemed to be a problem with each of them. The older son, Joe, and his wife had a baby 6 months after they were married and Joe had dropped out of college to work. Dick still felt the pain and distance which the early pregnancy and marriage had caused.

There were strong indications that their daughter, Sue, was a lesbian, but she wouldn't discuss it – and was cold toward her parents. Their second daughter, Jill, had dropped out of college to travel with a musical group which seemed like it was a cult. They seldom heard from her.

Their youngest child, Tom, was still at home because he was supposed to be finishing high school, but he had become involved in drugs and was often in trouble at school. Tom had several run-ins with the law. Whenever Dick tried to talk to Tom, they always ended up in an argument. And this was supposed to be a "Christian family"!

Dick alternated between feeling sorry for himself and being angry at the whole world – God included. He had troubles before, but now everything was falling apart at the same time. And he was tired of it all. His stomach hurt and his chest felt tight. He seemed to live from weekend to weekend when he could grab a little extra rest. He didn't feel like working in the yard every Saturday any more. Rita crabbed that the yard was beginning to look shabby, but most of the time he just didn't care.

You can easily understand why Dick would feel he was failing in every important area of his life. You can also see areas he and Rita needed to work on to remedy the situation.

Now, what about your situation? Can you step back and look at it objectively, and then do your part to help bring about change where it's needed?

Midlife men generally have battles in the areas of self-esteem, the aging process, health issues, occupation, wife and family, and the place of God in their lives – plus the question, "What am I going to do with the rest of my life?" They need help in all these distress areas. Improvement in one area helps the others, but men need to process all of these areas. You can be an encourager and a facilitator – so your husband wins these battles.

ACCENTUATE THE POSITIVE
Your husband may be putting up a good front to you and

others – yet his self-esteem may be near zero. When he was younger and had more stamina, he could stand the stress – but now he is tired and everything is weighing him down all at once. He is less able to have a balanced view of himself.

You can help him feel better about himself by giving him lots of affirmation. You must be genuine, because he will quickly reject phoniness. He may outwardly reject your genuine compliments and praise, yet inwardly he will be storing up your affirming words. He may feel negative about lots of areas of his life, and may not give you any indication that your positive affirmations are doing him any good. But they are adding up inside, and when he comes through his midlife transition, he will openly appreciate your encouragement and positive help.

When every area of his life looks messed up, you can build his confidence by helping him see his strong points. Point out how much he has grown over the years. Let him see how his personality and talents are being used – and will continue to be used in his occupation, and with his family and friends. If you believe in him – he will find it easier to believe in himself.

ELIMINATE THE NEGATIVE

Picture two marriages: one marriage the wife affirms her husband, while in the second marriage the wife destroys her husband by only majoring on his faults, with frequent criticism, and ridicule. Now decide which marriage you want to have a part in forming. Eliminate negative remarks to your husband, or about him. Adopt a "build-and-support- only" policy.

An extra benefit from your campaign of focusing on his good points is that you will increasingly appreciate him. You will continue to find more strong qualities about him – so you will have more to compliment him about. The opposite is also true. When you begin to pick on your husband's faults, you will soon *only see his bad points.* Everything about him will seem wrong.

That is one reason why the divorce process gets so ugly. In order to legally support a divorce, the husband and wife each have to point out the faults in their mate. Soon they see nothing but bad. Even when some couples would like to stop the proceedings and restore their marriage, one or both of them has majored on the other's faults so strongly that contempt is the only feeling left. Remember to practice your "build-and-support-only" policy.

AT PEACE WITH HIS BODY

You can't keep your husband's body from getting older, but you can help him feel good about his physical appearance. Instead of making remarks about the paunch around his waist or his graying hair, you can tell him how attractive he is to you. Remember that many younger women are fascinated by older men. Look at your husband through the eyes of a twenty-five-year-old and see what characteristics she would admire about him. Then be sure to tell him specifically the ways in which he looks good to you. Sally used to say to me (Jim), "I really like your tight buns." It feels good to be admired by your wife!

Encourage your husband to have a good medical exam. He may not have done so for years – if ever. At midlife, men begin to worry about symptoms they previously ignored. Some men become almost obsessed with the possibility of dying early. They fear heart attacks and other serious ailments. They know they're in the time of life when such illnesses are more likely to occur.

A thorough physical examination will put your husband's mind at rest, or show him what needs to be remedied, problems which might become serious or prevented, or lessened if detected.

You can, of course, help your husband's health by providing nutritious meals and especially by keeping down his calorie intake. I know its fun to cook, and bake all those yummy dishes, but you're not helping him by overfeeding him. In fact, you increase his risk of heart attack and other problems. He also may need vitamin and mineral supplements during this time of extra stress. For example, there is strong evidence that a lack in B vitamins contributes to fatigue, depression, irritability, anxiety, confusion, and restlessness.

"Wow!" I hear you exclaim, "I'm going to get some vitamin B right now and get my husband straightened out!"

Before you get too excited, remember that vitamins are not a cure-all. They are worth trying, however, as an aid to better health. During my (Jim) midlife crisis my physician recommended that I take a high potency vitamin B capsule, plus eat a healthier diet. There's lots of information on the Internet to help you with healthier eating. Consider eating more raw food, eliminating as much sugar as possible, eliminate carbonated drinks, and reduce the amount of protein he gets through meat products. There are many websites which will help you move toward eating a healthier diet, look on the internet for "raw food diets."

Also encourage your husband to start an exercise program.

Do something which doesn't create extra work. Daily walking is easier and cheaper than joining a gym which requires special clothes, an extra trip – and maybe another obligation. Perhaps you can find something the two of you like to do. That could be part of the extra time you spend with each other.

Also help him get sufficient rest. The pressure he is under will be somewhat easier, and problems won't seem as big if he is not physically tired. Rest comes not only from the hours he spends in bed, but also from leisure activities where he can set aside his cares for a while. You can help by *not* planning jobs for him, or by not discussing heavy matters every time he gets a chance to sit down.

WORK WEIGHTS

Your husband is probably fighting some battles is his occupation. Often midlife men are dissatisfied with their work. Some fear losing their jobs. Still others are simply tired of working so hard. Be alert to whatever your husband expresses about work and encourage him to talk more.

If he is dissatisfied with his job, help him think through alternatives. Let him know you support him if he decides to change jobs. Sometimes men don't actually end up making major job changes, but knowing you are on his side, if he wanted to change, will relieve part of the pressure.

The fear of losing his job may be real or imagined. When he is depressed, he may inaccurately sense that his job is being threatened. Perhaps you can give him a better perception of the true situation.

If your husband needs to cut down on the amount of work, or make a change, encourage him to think this through cautiously. His self-esteem will suffer more if he makes hasty, unwise decisions which he may later regret. Let him bounce ideas off you as together you both consider the advantages and disadvantages of a job change. Perhaps he could use the help from books such as, *What Color Is Your Parachute?* [1] This book has been on the *New York Times* bestseller list for many years and will give good insights on how to change careers wisely.

Whatever your husband's occupation, you should be interested in what he is doing. He may be in a field where you have absolutely no talent and little knowledge, but you can encourage him to share as much as is appropriate with you. He can at least tell you his feelings and how the job affects him. Some work is the type where you can be involved. If that is appropriate, do what you can to make yourself available to help your husband.

Whether or not his occupation is one in which you can be involved, be his ally and best friend as he works through whatever job struggles he may be having. Let him know you are with him, and you would be willing to modify your life-style, if he decides it is best to change, or cut down.

We know some families who have moved into smaller housing so the husband could cut back on his work hours. In other family situations wives have gone to work outside the home to help with income when their husbands changed to lower-paying jobs, returned to school for more training – or when the couple decided to take the big leap of starting their own business.

WILL HE STAY?

We want to clearly state, "Your husband's decision to stay, or not to stay, will not be determined alone by your actions and attitudes!" Some women feel that we are suggesting that a man's decision to stay in the marriage is totally dependent on what the wife does or doesn't do. This is absolutely not true! Your husband is a big boy and he has the ability to make choices. However, we have found that the wife plays a very large role in helping the husband decide to work on the marriage.

Your husband is also wrestling with the issue of where his family fits into his life. As we have said, this era has a high divorce rate. Many midlife divorces could be avoided if husbands and the wives worked together on their midlife problems.

Remind yourself that your midlife husband must evaluate *every* part of his life. Deciding whether or not he is going to stay married to you is one of the necessary, but often fearful, or tearful, processes. Some men quickly decide that they want the marriage to continue – with some improvements. But for others, the decision is more of a struggle.

Ultimately, your husband will have to answer this question himself. Your part is to pray for God to work in him, and to encourage him by understanding – and meeting his needs! Plus, do your own growing and changing so that you are more interesting to your husband.

Frequently, I (Jim) ask women how they are doing in the three areas which midlife men complain about.

1. Midlife men complain that their wives are "naggy", controlling, and often boss them around like children (sometimes

men do act like children).

2. Midlife men complain that their wives are overweight, out of shape, and do not care about physical appearance. Remember, men are very visual, and when their wife looks good to them, that translates that she is interested in sex. A high priority in a man's life is regular, exciting sex for which he doesn't have to beg.

3. Midlife men complain that their wives have not had a new thought since they got married. They complain that their wives are not growing intellectually or in their careers, which makes them very dependent clingy people. Lack of growth often is negative to a midlife man. How are you doing in these three areas?

We would like to say optimistically that each of you will be a winner with your husband in this struggle. Realistically, though, we know that some of you are on the verge of losing the battle – and others of you have already lost.

The problem is that there are two of you involved in the decision, and you can't make your husband do what he will not do. Our hearts ache for those of you who have a breaking, or broken marriage. We wish it were in our powers to give each of you a whole and happy relationship with your husbands.

If after all of the changes we have suggested in this book, your husband still decides he must get out of the marriage – then your job is to build a complete and healthy life for you and your family in this new reality. Part of that new reality is to remember that a divorce decree does not necessarily mean that your marriage is over. We have known a number of couples who have divorced each other multiple times, and yet have remarried and are still together. But let's look objectively at the situation.

Women express two common types of reactions when a marriage breaks up. Some women never let go of their rage and blame toward their husbands. These women have a difficult and longtime recovery process. Other women have given the marriage their very best shot – they have grown and changed so the previous complaints of their husbands have been eliminated. Still their husband walked away. These second group of women leave with sadness, but without guilt, because they have done their best before God. You will find additional help in one of our other books – *Moving On After He Moves Out.*[2]

THE STALL

For those of you whose husbands have not actually divorced you, I want to encourage you not to give up hope. Many men verbally threaten divorce, as a way to pressure their wife to change, but do not actually start legal proceedings. Others go so far as to start proceedings, but then delay the process. We have found that often these men really do not want a divorce. Don't push them into hurrying up the procedure as time and patience allows a chance for restoration to take place. Many midlife husbands are in utter confusion. They don't know what they want.

If there is another woman in the picture, she may be pushing your husband into divorcing you. But he may also be having second thoughts about whether he wants to get married to the "other woman," or anyone. If you want to preserve your marriage, do what you can to stall the divorce process. And in the meantime do the good, positive things you can to win back your husband.

THE GIRLFRIEND ROLE

If your husband has left you, or if he is having an affair, relate to him as if you were in the dating stage once again. Behave as if you were his girlfriend. That means you don't make any demands on him, you are on your best behavior around him, you dress to attract him, you do whatever it was that "rang his bells" during your dating days.

He doesn't want a hovering mother, or a nagging wife. He yearns for the exhilaration of a girlfriend. If you provide that, then he is less likely to seek it elsewhere. That is also a good attitude for you to take even if your marriage is not so threatened.

You might be helped to know some other traits men *do like* – and *don't like* in women.

Men *DO* like:
- A sense of humor – adds fun to everyday life, no matter how hectic
- Kindness, and gentleness
- They like makeup if they don't know you have it on – or at least if it is natural enough to look real
- A good figure, but curves, not only thinness
- They are drawn to vitality and aliveness – but not to the woman who is the "life of the party" for other men
- They appreciate tact in a woman – her talent to smooth hectic situations
- Most of all they like a woman who makes life seem easy and uncomplicated

Men _DON'T_ like:
- Cattiness, snide remarks about other people – it makes you look insecure
- They do not like new styles at first, but usually like them after they become accustomed to them
- They hate complaining, but enjoy chatter if it's humorous and interesting
- They do not like the siren type, she makes them feel uneasy
- They do not like to hear about your former conquests
- They have a horror of becoming involved in long, emotional discussions
- Generally, they do not like candlelight at the dinner table, but men succumb when the mood is relaxing, and good conversation goes along with it. Otherwise, they want to see their food clearly so they can concentrate on it
- Fretting drives them crazy

CHANGING OF THE GUARD

At midlife, there are some aspects of family life to which your husband may have trouble adapting – but he must. Role changes take place with a midlife couple's parents and with their children. By this age it is clear that our parents are no longer our protectors, we are the final authority over how we live our lives. The world now belongs to the midlife generation. We have to control our own lives; our parents cannot do it for us. Parents cannot watch out for us, and we don't want them to. Yet there is a feeling of loss when we realize no one is going to care for us.

Family power-plays escalate when a married couple goes through the midlife years. When an elderly parent tries to control you, they often are doing it to bolster their own sense of insecurity. Similarly you may try to pressure your teenage and young adult children. You may not feel malicious when you do this, but you may be putting on pressure because of your own fear of losing control.

You feel you aren't needed by your children as much anymore – those uncomfortable new feelings just don't seem right to your world. A midlife man may be unaware of changes between his kids and himself until it's almost too late – then he is stunned by how differently everyone now looks at each other. If you and your husband can talk about these changes in your children, and your parents, then the adjustments will be less dramatic.

SPIRITUAL DECISIONS

At midlife a man generally takes a new look at his spiritual life. Some solid Christian men wrestle with doubts and questions which never occurred to them before, or that they thought they had settled earlier. They wonder about God's genuine care for them, His sovereignty, and the value of keeping moral standards. Some men grow cold or careless in their contact with God, or gradually withdraw from any connections with God. I (Jim) had a very deep spiritual struggle during my midlife crisis – I'm glad that Sally, and God, did not give up on me. To read more about my struggle and recovery look at our book, *Men in Midlife Crisis*.[3]

Other men, who have never been believers, find God for the first time. Some men go back to their childhood religious experience, hoping to find solace and direction there. One man we know decided once again to follow his Jewish faith, after he had ignored it for years. He became so committed that sadly his wife divorced him!

If you are a committed Christian, you are no doubt eager for your husband to experience a true, vital relationship with Jesus Christ, whether he is already a Christian or not. You know that your lives will be the very best when both of you are walking in the power and joy of the Lord. That is a commendable desire, but be careful! Many zealous wives have mistakenly felt they were doing God's will by forcing their husband into a spiritual decision. It *is* God's will for your husband to be a Christian, and to live as one. But it *is not* God's will for you to force that commitment on your husband.

Even the best Christian husband will have trouble swallowing a super-pious attitude from you while he is struggling with the swirling issues of his midlife crisis. Remember, he feels that he is failing in everything, and if you are throwing around all your spirituality, he is going to be sickened by it. You may be receiving neat insights from the Bible, but be careful how you share them with your husband. Keep learning from the Lord, but also ask God to control when, how, and if you should talk about it with your husband. First Peter 3:1 teaches that husbands will more likely be influenced by "godly lives" than by words.

GOD CAN BE TRUSTED

Your husband will need to make his own decision about how he is going to relate to God. You can whet his appetite by your personal spiritual life, but you can't force him. Let God be the one to do the convincing. God's Spirit working quietly inside him will do more good than all the noise you make from the outside. You can claim the principle of Philippians 2:13 to work for your husband's spiritual life, "For God [not a wife] is working in you, giving you the desire and the power to do what pleases him."

If your husband is a Christian and he is wavering, take hope in the assurance of Philippians 1: 6, "God, who began the good work within you, will continue his work until it is finally finished on the day when Christ Jesus returns." You can pray with faith for your husband when he perhaps is too weak to pray for himself.

There were times when Jim didn't have any emotional energy left to pray for the help he needed. It was as if his life was a car with a dead battery, flat tires, and no gas. When I (Sally) sensed those times, I prayed instead of him and claimed the promises he would have claimed if he had the strength.

Spiritual decisions have to be made in the inner person. Your husband will arrive at his own level of faith and commitment to God as a result of his personal response to God's work within him. Although you cannot force the outcome of his decision, you can be an influence by your prayers and winsome life. God promises that your supportive presence will be a help to your man, "Two people can accomplish more than twice as much as one; they get a better return for their labor. If one person falls, the other can reach out and help. But people who are alone when they fall are in real trouble" (Ecclesiastes 4:9-10).

If your husband has been gone from your home, but now it looks as if he may come back, you may have many questions about how to relate to him. In the next chapter we'll share a conversation with one woman who faced such a situation.

Was it for nothing that I kept my heart pure and kept myself from doing wrong? All I get is trouble all day long; every morning brings the pain. Then I realized how bitter I had become, how pained I had been by all I had seen. I was so foolish and ignorant – I must have seemed like a senseless animal to you. Yet I still belong to use; you are holding my right hand. Whom have I in heaven but you? (Psalms 73:13-14, 21-25)

18

AIDING HIS REENTRY

Billie asked me (Sally) to help her. Her husband left for another woman – and cut all connections with the church, neighbors, and other friends.

She began, "I've talked to you a lot about my fear that my husband would never come back. Well, over the past few months we have been talking a lot. And the last 3 weeks he's been at the house for several meals. Now I'm afraid, because I'm not sure what to do. He seems to be coming back. How do I handle it all? What are our friends and neighbors going to think, since he so strongly rejected them?"

She paused, then added, "I have a whole new batch of questions and problems that I didn't have before. I thought it would be easy – Vince would give up his girlfriend, come home – and that would be that. But now I see that it's even more complicated than his leaving. What do I do?

REALITY

A husband's reentry often can be almost as difficult as his

leaving. Many new adaptations are needed. Neither of you are dealing with the same old circumstances – or the same people. Each person has grown and changed. It's a whole new mix. Be careful not to make assumptions that simply because he comes through the front door with his suitcase, everything is automatically going to be like the "good old days."

In fact, if everything does go back to the "good old days" then the two of you will be in trouble again. Remember, the circumstances of the "good old days" partially caused your husband to leave, so hopefully the change in everyone will result in a more satisfying marriage for both of you.

Some cautions at this point are necessary. Don't be overly anxious to have him back. Be sure the decision is his. Make sure he is not being pressured or coerced – or that he is returning against his will. On the other hand, also make sure you don't become his doormat. It would be better if he stayed away a little longer and thoroughly worked through his problems. Perhaps he needs a counselor, so that when he comes back he is ready to do the necessary work to make the marriage great – not just a survival contest.

EATING HUMBLE PIE

One of the big reentry problems for the husband is "loss of face." When he left, he may have burned lots of bridges, thinking he will never be back, nor would he have to relate to certain people again. He may have cut himself off from neighbors, people at church, and other friends when he started his new life-style. As he tries to make his way back, he likely will feel humiliated. He may feel pressured to constantly give explanations, or say he was a "Jerk."

At this point a wife can be very helpful – or she can stick the knife into him. If she feels that he ought to make public apologies, or come crawling back on his hands and knees, begging her forgiveness – then she is likely to exploit the situation, and enjoy her position of power. He may feel too battered to go through the humiliation, and she will probably lose him again.

She can, however, make it easy for her husband to return. When he visits one night for dinner, she could make it convenient for him to hang around. They could go for a walk and express affection through flirting, laughing, occasional touching and hugging – but not clutchiness with a sense of "Aha! I have him now!" Rather, "It's just good to be together!" Then she could suggest, "Since it's late, maybe you'd like to just sleep over – you could use the guest room. We'll set the alarm, and you can be up and showered before the kids are awake, so they don't get any wrong ideas that you're moving back permanently. I also want you to know that if you sleep over tonight that doesn't mean I think you're going to move back. It's just that I like to be with you."

If your husband decides to move back, the two of you must talk about how to handle neighbors, friends, and church people. Maybe you'll even decide to have a small dinner party, or cookout to let people see you together again. Most couples, however, let the word get around quietly, spearheaded mostly by the wife who shares the simple information in a positive way, "It's good to have my husband back again, and he's so glad to be back." There may be some sticky relationships, but as the couple talks together about how to handle them and invites God to be involved in the process, they will find that most people are delighted that their marriage has been reunited.

NO FENCE-SITTING

Another problem created by reentry is the husband's need to cut off his old relationships in the single world as he moves back into the marriage. Once again he has the problem of losing face. He may have told people he was getting a divorce, and he may have dated several women.

This "other woman" detour has to stop – as he returns to the main highway. The reentry will not be successful if the husband tries to keep one foot on two roads. That's why it's important for him to be sure he really wants to be back. He must make a clean break with his "temporary bachelorhood." A wife can be supportive, but she must be careful not to nag him – she can't do it for him. He is the one to tell the singles that he is back with his family. She can help best by praying and encouraging him so he feels strong enough to make the break.

In our book, *Men in Midlife Crisis,* [1] I (Jim) talk about how to get out of an affair, and that affairs break up because they are not meeting a person's needs. When a husband's affair reaches the point where the affair is no longer satisfying, he will probably evaluate what he really wants in life – this is a continuation of the prioritizing of his needs and values. When he decides to return home, it will help his adjustment if he makes a clean break with any women he has dated in his short-lived single life.

PRACTICALITIES

After I (Sally) had talked generally with Billie about her husband's reentry, she was still loaded with questions – such as, "Will I ever be able to trust him?"

"Billie, remember how trust grew the first time? When you

first met, you didn't have a full-grown relationship of trust. Your trust grew as you spent more time with each other and learned about each other. Trust will return again by the same process. Remember, you and your husband are not alone – God is involved and is going to be strengthening and guiding each of you."

"What if, after he's moved everything back into the house, I find an old note or a ticket stub from a date he had while he was gone? Do I confront him with it?"

"No, forget it, and certainly don't read the note – it will only cause you more pain. It's part of the past! You've forgiven him. You've decided to make a new start in your marriage. Let that old thing die! Commit it to God's care. You may be tempted to distrust Vince, especially if you see an old note or ticket stub. Those small things may cause you to feel anger, or depression – but you must let go of it. In a quick prayer tell God, 'I found this note, and it could tear me up – but I choose to surrender it to you, and trust you to continue to heal our marriage. I am dropping this note into the trash – as I visualize that you are now running it through your holy "garbage disposal".'"

"What if *she* calls again – or writes a letter?" Billie grimaced.

"Assure Vince that you love him – but let him handle her. It's his responsibility to make the break with his past. Also, ask God to meet the needs of the other woman, so she doesn't keep trying to take Vince away."

"What if *he* gets restless and wants to go again?"

"Remember that the reentry transition is likely to take several months or even a year or more. When you first met Vince, you were not ready to get married, and when you were first married, you needed time to adjust to living together. An adjustment period is necessary now. During this time he may feel restless. Assure him – if he needs to go for a ride, he should feel free to do that. If he needs to be alone in the house, provide that opportunity. Or if he wants you to go someplace just with him – go. And continually trust him to God during this reentry transition."

Then Billie said, "I've changed a lot since he left. I'm more independent. Do I change back to becoming dependent again?"

"No, one of the things attracting Vince back to you is that you've done some growing – you're more interesting, as well as independent. He likes you better this way. Remember, he's also changed. Talk about how you've each changed – so you can adapt to your new selves."

"Sometimes," I continued, "a wife has been so cautious in dealing with her husband during the early stages of his midlife crisis – that she has never told him any of her personal feelings. If the marriage is to work again, you and your husband must both share your feelings. That doesn't mean that on the first night he comes back you dump everything on him. But it does mean that you increasingly share who you are – and how you've changed. You need to share what you feel, and what's going on inside of you. This permission to share doesn't mean you bring up the past separation time. It does mean you share who you are now, and what God has been doing to you."

MORE VITAL ISSUES

Billie then brought up the subject of their children. "The kids are happy about the prospects of Vince's return, but they're afraid it might only be temporary."

"You can dispel their fears by telling them that God loves each of them. Tell them that Dad has been struggling with some problems – but he is working things out. Calm them by saying, 'It looks as if we're going to be a family again.' Also assure them that Dad loves each of them – and so do you. Tell them that God is going to continue to care for your entire family."

Then Billie said, "Sometimes I wake up in the middle of the night crying – because he's having sex with the other woman. Now I ask myself, 'What will it be like the first time we have sex?' Will that 'other woman' nightmare cause me to be frigid? How can I ever give myself to him again?"

"When you first met, you didn't jump into bed. You had months and months of getting to know each other, and expressing care and tenderness for each other. Then, after you were married, it was an easy passionate step to sexual intercourse. Follow that same pattern now. Tell him frankly about your fears, and also tell him you don't want your fears to put him off – but you need a little time."

The "STD" ISSUES

Also, this is the time to talk about STDs (sexually transmitted diseases). It's not an issue of whether the two of you are building a new love relationship, it's an issue of whether either of you are carrying STDs. We are not just dealing with two people anymore – it is now an issue of the sexual history of any person that you or your husband might have slept with during your separation. Plus, what is the sexual history of all of the various partners, and partners of partners? It would be extremely normal for both of you to have complete physical examinations and be thoroughly tested for STDs and AIDS. Until both of you have been tested and received clear test reports, it would be vital to use a condom so you do not risk your future health.

Counselors, who work with reconnecting couples, say that sexual problems are very common. So counselors ask the couple to agree with some basics. *First*, they both agreed that they would not have sexual intercourse, until they both equally desired it. Until then, the relationship would be one of hugging, kissing, assuring each other, building each other's emotional strength, petting, and touching – but no guilt or pressure for sex. This freedom from obligation allows the emotions to be free. In the setting of growing trust and greater expression of love and caring, the old sexual desires will fully return.

"Can I forgive him after all I've been through?"

"Yes, you can, because God has forgiven you for your part in the marriage troubles. Yes you can forgive – because it's not only about you – Vince was deeply hurt in the marriage as well as you! You can forgive Vince because your children need you to forgive him. You must forgive him because – unless you do – he will be lonely again – and there are thousands of women waiting to meet his needs. If you hold onto your unforgiving spirit to protect yourself from hurt, you will be hurt again!

"If you hold onto your unforgiveness, so you have a club to hit him with later – then that club will beat your marriage to death. You will use it for every unrelated minor sin your husband commits for the rest of his life. Billie, you must decide to ask God to forgive you for any part you had in your marital problems, and ask God to give you the grace to forgive Vince. Then forgive him totally, and give up completely all of your rights to ever bring it up again."

You can see from this conversation that there will be many adjustments if your husband comes home again, but this homecoming is what you have wanted more than anything else! The realignment period may not be easy, but keep focused on the promise of good years ahead – and God's strength to make it happen.

> **Who dares accuse us whom God has chosen for his own? Can anything ever separate us from Christ's love? Does it mean he no longer loves us if we have troubles or calamities? No, despite all these things, overwhelming victory is ours through Christ, who loved us. (Romans 8:33-38)**

19

You Can Do This!!

For most men – and their wives – the midlife crisis can be the most difficult life experience they have had so far. More changes are taking place in a shorter period of time than ever before. And at the same time the man is confronted with aging, plus his need for a reevaluation of every area of his life. He is undergoing giant upheavals, many of them losses, at a time when he is less emotionally and physically able to handle the stress.

Many young adults ask what they can do to prevent a midlife crisis. We tell them that midlife cannot be avoided any more than a teenager can avoid being a teenager. But young couples can prepare themselves now, so the crisis is less severe, and so they will be more apt to come through it successfully.

To minimize some of the stresses, the young adult should select an occupation which matches abilities and interests. Some young people get pushed into a profession which pleases the parents, or some other influential person – but it's not in line with the person or the gifts God has given. Sometimes a person gets locked into a job because it provides the income for the moment, but it may not be what he really wants to do for the rest of his life. He may even put up with it for years, but at midlife an ill-suited job will greatly increase his stress.

Problem areas should be worked out as they arise, not ignored until they become monumental at midlife when everything else is happening. Couples should learn to communicate frequently and adequately, but most of all they should meet each other's needs. Unmet needs in the marriage relationship are like a tooth cavity – until you fix the cavity, there's going to be lots of pain.

HOPE FOR THE FUTURE

The exciting thing is that once the midlife transition has been successfully completed, there is a better life ahead. We are not saying this simply to encourage you through a rough time – or because Christians are supposed to be optimistic. Once a man has settled most of the pressing midlife issues – his aging, occupation, his marriage, and identity issues – he will enter a long, peaceful period which generally is extremely productive.

The post midlife man is more optimistic about life in general. He sees that his wisdom and experience are as valuable as his physical strength were in his youth. He is generally more congenial at work. Instead of feeling competitive with younger men, he now becomes their teacher and coach. He enjoys passing to others what he knows. He now helps others succeed. He chooses and keeps friends on the basis of mutual appreciation, rather than what they can do for him. He becomes a gentler, mellow man. As a husband, he is more tender and thoughtful. He is also a better lover and takes time to be sentimental and romantic.

Sally and I know from our own experience that these good changes really do happen! They happened for us, and we know other couples who have also experienced these good results after the midlife crisis. Marriages can become stronger and more satisfying if you both "hang on" during the rough times, rather than throwing in the towel and giving up on your marriage. Many marriages have been restored after couples have been separated for months or even years. Couples once again enjoy the fun of a truly happy, satisfying relationship with each other.

During these trying midlife times keep focused on the concepts in this Bible verse – "But in all these things we overwhelmingly conquer through Him who loved us" (Romans 8:37 New International Version). The word "conqueror" suggests that there was a battle. The battle wasn't won by God doing all of the work – you had to do your part and make your changes. The battle had to be fought, but it was won – God was with you!

GOD'S TIME OR OUR TIME

I (Jim) have always had a definite idea when God should do things. In the process of trying to control the events in my life – I sometimes find that I am trying to control God. Or even worse, I may begin to think that God is my servant – and I'm God!

I struggle most in two areas. First, I don't know why God allows certain things to happen in our lives. The second area where I struggle is a matter of timing, "Why doesn't God do things when I think they should be done?"

There is a wonderful story in the Bible found in the gospel of John Chapter 11. This account graphically portrays the confusion I often feel when God doesn't work on my time schedule. Allow me to quote part of this chapter to you.

A man named Lazarus was sick. He lived in Bethany with his sisters, Mary and Martha. Their brother, Lazarus, was sick. So the two sisters sent a message to Jesus telling Him, "Lord, the one you love is very sick." (John 11:1, 3 NIV) [1]

But when Jesus heard about it he said, 'Lazarus's sickness is not unto death. No, it is for the glory of God. I, the son of God, will receive glory from this.' Although Jesus loved Martha, Mary, and Lazarus, he stayed where he was for the next two days and did not go to them. (John 11:4-5 NIV) [2]

This is where I frequently have trouble in my spiritual life. I have it all planned how God is supposed to work things out in my life. When he doesn't, I am not only disappointed, but sometimes angry. There may be times during this Midlife experience when you also will be disappointed with God, because he is not working on your time schedule. This story shows us the hope!

The account continues with Jesus going to the burial site of Lazarus. There he confronts people who do not believe in miracles, he also comforts the two sisters of Lazarus – then he proceeds to raise Lazarus from the dead.

I want you to clearly understand the important lessons in this story:
1. *God does not always work on our time schedule – he wants us to trust him.*
2. *God expects us to do what we can do in the process of marriage recovery.*

3. *God expects us to then continue walking in the new healed marriage patterns which we have learned by going through Midlife Crisis.*

When Jesus arrived at the tomb of Lazarus, there was a large stone rolled across the opening. He told the people, *"Role the stone aside."*[3] Martha objected saying, *"Lord, by now the smell will be terrible because he has been dead for four days."* Jesus responds, *"Didn't I tell you that you will see God's glory if you believe?"*[4] So the people rolled the stone away. Are you ever caught in that position where you are afraid to act because you can't believe in miracles?

I firmly believe that if the people had not responded by rolling the stone away, Jesus would not have raised Lazarus from the dead. He was waiting to see a demonstration of their faith, by doing what they could – roll the stone away.

Bluntly, let me ask you, "What are the things you should be doing to prepare the way for God to do the miracle in your marriage?" Make a list of the "stones" you need to roll away in this process of marriage resurrection.

When the people responded in faith, then Jesus called Lazarus to come out of the tomb. The tomb was a deep pit in the ground with more than thirty steps down to the bottom. Lazarus came hopping up the steps totally bound in grave clothes.

I've always wondered, "If Jesus can raise a dead man, why didn't he also take off the grave clothes?" It's the same issue as "rolling the stone away." God is not going to do what you can and should be doing – but he certainly will do the miracles which only He can do! To me, unwrapping the grave clothing is a picture of the continued process of healing and restoration of your marriage – even after you have gotten back together.

> And the Lord himself, the king of Israel, will live among you! At last your troubles will be over, and you will fear disaster no more. He is a mighty Savior. He will rejoice over you with great gladness. With his love, he will calm all your fears. He will exalt over you by singing a happy song. I will gather you who mourn for the appointed festivals; you will be disgraced no more. (Zephaniah 3:15-18)

God has a miracle for you – but he waits for you to roll the stone away. After your marriage has started to come back to life, God will depend on you to continue the unwrapping process, by consistent changes and growth.

Again, let me assure you – "You Can Do This!"

It has been a wonderful privilege to walk with you as together we have thought about practical ways to restore your marriage. All of us involved in this ministry, will all be praying for you as you continue this difficult, but wonderful experience of your marriage being restored. Also remember that we are available to help you through our chat rooms, and through personal counseling. Our website is www.midlife.com.

I wish you God's greatest blessing on your life and your marriage.

Jim Conway, Kona, HI and Conway, MI 2010,
(revising editor for this book)
President and Founder, Midlife Dimensions, Inc.

Jim Conway, Ph.D. and Sally Conway, M.S. started *Midlife Dimensions / Christian Living Resources*, to minister to the midlife family around the world through Books, counseling, radio / TV programs, audio and videotapes, films, and seminars.

Jim continues the Ministry even after Sally's death in 1997.

If you would like more information about Seminars, Books and publications, media, personal counseling, or about the Chat Rooms, log on to our website at:

www.midlife.com
Contact us by email at
Conway@midlife.com
Or write to us at Midlife Dimensions at
P.O. Box 505 Conway, Michigan 49770
Or
P.O. Box 92860 Norco, California 92860

Part 5
Chapter Notes

CHAPTER ONE
1. Jim Conway, *Men in Midlife Crisis* (Elgin, IL: David C. Cook Publishing Co., 1978),

CHAPTER TWO
1. Daniel J. Levinson, et al., *The Seasons of a Man's Life* (New York: Ballantine Books, 1979).

2. Bernice L. Neugarten, ed., *Personality in Middle and Late Life* (New York: Atherton Press, 1964).

3. Roger L. Gould, *Transformation and Change in Adult Life* (Simon & Schuster, 1979).

4. Jim Conway, *Men in Midlife Crisis,* (David C. Cook, 1997).

5. Jim Conway, *Men in Midlife Crisis,* (David C. Cook, 1997),

6. Jim Conway, *Men in Midlife Crisis,* (David C. Cook, 1997),

7. Jim Conway, *Men in Midlife Crisis,* (David C. Cook, 1997),

8. Edmund Bergler, *The Revolt of the Middle-Aged Man* (New York: A. A. Wynn, 1954, International Universities Press. Reprint edition, [September 1, 1985]). pp.

CHAPTER THREE
1. Daniel J. Levinson, et al., *The Seasons of a Man's Life*, (Ballantine Books: 1986) p. 199.

CHAPTER FOUR

1. William J. Lederer and Don D. Jackson, *The Mirages of Marriage* (New York, NY: 1994).

2. Jim Conway, *Men in Midlife Crisis* (David C. Cook, 1997).

3. Gail Sheehy, *Passages* (New York, NY: Ballantine, 2006).

4. Sheehy, *Passages.*

CHAPTER FIVE
1. Gail Sheehy, *Passages.*

CHAPTER SIX
1. Don Williams, *The Apostle Paul & Women in the Church* (Glendale, CA: Regal, 1977); Dorothy R. Pape, In *Search of God's ideal Woman* (Downers Grove, IL: InterVarsity Press, 1976); Richard and Joyce Boldrey, *Chauvinist or Feminist? Paul's View of Women* (Grand Rapids, MI: Baker Book House, 1976); Letha Scanzoni and Nancy Hardesty, *All Were Meant to be* (Waco, TX: Word Books, 1974); Herbert and Fern Harrington Miles, *Husband-Wife Equality* (Old Tappan, NJ: Fleming H. Revell, 1978).

CHAPTER SEVEN
1. To learn more about Bill and Pam Farrel's ministries visit: www.farrelcommunications.com

CHAPTER EIGHT

1. Vital Statistics of the U.S., U.S. Dept. of Health, Education, & Welfare, Health Statistics, 2004.

2. Ruth Myers, ***31 Days of Praise (Multnomah Publishers, Inc. 2002)***

3. Robert F. Winch, *Mate Selection: A Study of Complementary Needs* (New York, NY: Harper, 1958, 1974). Irvington Publishers (June 1, 1974).

CHAPTER NINE

1. Jim Conway, *Adult Children of Legal or Emotional Divorce* (Downers Grove, IL: Intervarsity Press).

2. *New Living Translation.* Unless otherwise indicated, all Scripture quotations are taken from the Holy Bible, New Living Translation, copyright ©1996.

3. H. S. Vigenveno and Anne **Claire**, *Divorce and the Children* (Glendale, CA: Regal Books, 1979); H.

S. Vigenveno and Anne **Claire**, *No One Gets Divorced Alone* (Ventura, CA: Regal Books, 1987).

Guidelines for Building a Happy, Harmonious Single-Parent Home by H. S. Vigenveno and Anne Claire are so practical and helpful that we are including them here. They are useful for two-parent homes, too!

Basic Attitudes – What atmosphere do we want to create in our home?

1. What is our main emphasis as a family? How will we change or strengthen this?

2. What am I telling the world and my children about myself by

my life-style? How will I change or strengthen this?

3. What memories will we have as a result of living together in a single-parent home?

4. How can we become better listeners to each other?

5. Do we allow each other freedom of speech and the right to express different opinions?

6. Is our home a place of love? Of respect? Of courtesy? Of good manners?

Standards and Rules – Does everybody know what is expected as a member of this family?

1. What time is bedtime on school nights? On weekends?

2. How much television time is allowed each day?

3. How much time do we need for homework? How much should Mom or Dad get involved in homework?

4. What books and magazines will we have in our home? What reading material will not be permitted?

5. What family standards will we adopt for videos, movies, and the internet?

6. How will we handle issues such as alcohol, cigarette smoking, drugs, etc.?

7. What freedoms will teens have?

8. When an adult is not at home, are the children and teenagers allowed to invite their friends into the house? Girls? Boys?

9. Do we agree on standards for clothes, hair, and language? What compromises will we make?

10. What are our nutritional standards? Should we make any changes?

11. Do we say grace before meals at home, and in restaurants?

The Parent's Responsibilities – What do I need to do to help my children mature?

1. How can I help my children be prepared for adulthood by the time they are legally adults?

2. How can I teach self-reliance?

3. What are my guidelines for discipline?

4. How will I reinforce good behavior? Discipline bad behavior?

5. How can I help my children develop their individual interests?

6. How can I deal with boredom when a child complains there is nothing to do?

7. How will my children get their spending money – by allowance – by need – or by earning it?

8. How will household responsibilities be delegated inside the house – in the yard – training, feeding and cleaning up after pets, etc.?

Parental Guidelines – Am I prepared to lead my family with these guidelines?

1. Will we attend church as a family? How many church activities can we handle as a family? As individuals?

2. Will we have family devotions – and encourage personal devotions?

3. What will our weekends be like? How much time will we set

aside for chores? Family activities? Individual activities?

4. How will we celebrate birthdays? Holidays? Have I considered my children's mother / father, grandparents, aunts, uncles and other relatives on special days of the year?

5. Am I able to handle my finances? Should I budget my money? Can I afford credit cards? Is it necessary to cut expenses?

6. Can I teach self-control by example? How can I strengthen my own self-control?

7. When will I discuss sex with my children? Am I prepared to answer their questions about sex?

8. Who can I turn to in times of crises for help?

CHAPTER TEN
1. John Powell, **The Secret of Staying in Love** (Niles, IL: Argus, 1974, 1995), pp. 64 – 66.

CHAPTER ELEVEN
1. James Dobson, **What Wives Wish Their Husbands Knew About Women** (Bordan, SK: Living Books, 1981).

2. www.msnbc.msn.com/id/10034785/.

3. Gladys Hunt, **MS Means Myself** (Grand Rapids, MI: Zondervan, 1972).

4. Archibald D. Hart, **Feeling Free** (Old Tappan, NJ: Revell, 1986).

CHAPTER TWELVE
1. John E. Gibson, "Can Humor Affect Friendship?" **Family Weekly (**February 24, 1980).

CHAPTER THIRTEEN

1. Robert J. Morgan, *Red Sea Rules: 10 God-Given Strategies for Difficult Times* (Nashville, TN: Thomas Nelson, 2001).

2. Philip Yancey, *Where Is God When It Hurts* (Grand Rapids: Zondervan, 1977, 1997).

3. Bruce Larson, *No Longer Strangers* (Waco, TX: Word Books, 1971, 1985).

CHAPTER FOURTEEN

1. Sally Conway, "Meditations of a Midlife Wife," unpublished poem, 1980.

2. Carole Jackson, *Color Me Beautiful* (NY, NY: Ballantine Books, 1987).

3. John Eldridge & Stasi Eldridge, *Captivating: Unveiling the Mystery of a Woman's Soul* (Nashville, TN: Thomas Nelson, 2005). Angela Thomas, *Do You Think I'm Beautiful?* (Nashville, TN: Thomas Nelson, 2005).

4. Ingrid Trobisch, *The Joy of Being a Woman* (New York: Harper & Row, 1975, 1995).

CHAPTER FIFTEEN

1. Jim Conway, *Men in Midlife Crisis* (Colorado Springs, CO: David C. Cook, 1997).

2. Sally Conway, Jim Conway, *When A Mate Wants Out* (Grand Rapids, MI: Zondervan Publishing House, 1992).

CHAPTER SIXTEEN

1. Jim and Sally Conway, *When a Mate Wants Out: Secrets for Saving a Marriage* (Grand Rapids, MI: Zondervan, 2000).

CHAPTER SEVENTEEN

1. Richard Nelson Bolles, *What Color Is Your Parachute? 2009: A Practical Manual for Job-Hunters and Career-Changers.* (San Francisco, CA: Ten Speed, 2008).

2. Jim and Sally Conway, *Moving on After He moves Out* (Downers Grove, IL: Intervarsity Press, 1995).

3. Jim and Sally Conway, *Men In Midlife Crisis* (Colorado Springs, CO: David C. Cook, 1997).

CHAPTER EIGHTEEN

1. Jim and Sally Conway, *Men In Midlife Crisis* (Colorado Springs, CO: David C. Cook, 1997).

CHAPTER NINETEEN

1. John 11:1, 3 NIV
2. John 11:4, 5 NIV
3. John 11:38
4. John 11:39-40

Publishing That Works For You

Do you need a speaker?

Do you want Jim Conway to speak to your group or event? Then contact Larry Davis at: **(623) 337-8710** or email: **ldavis@intermediapr.com** or use the contact form at: **www.intermediapr.com**.

Whether you want to purchase bulk copies of *Your Husband's Midlife Crisis* or buy another book for a friend, get it now at: **www.imprbooks.com**.

If you have a book that you would like to publish, contact Terry Whalin, Publisher, at Intermedia Publishing Group, (623) 337-8710 or email: twhalin@intermediapub.com or use the contact form at: www.intermediapub.com.